HEAVY
BURDENS

HEAVY BURDENS

SEVEN WAYS LGBTQ CHRISTIANS
EXPERIENCE HARM IN THE CHURCH

BRIDGET EILEEN RIVERA

BrazosPress

a division of Baker Publishing Group
Grand Rapids, Michigan

Published by Brazos Press
a division of Baker Publishing Group
PO Box 6287, Grand Rapids, MI 49516-6287
www.brazospress.com

Printed in the United States of America

Library of Congress Cataloging-in-Publication Data
Names: Rivera, Bridget Eileen, 1989– author.
Title: Heavy burdens : seven ways LGBTQ Christians experience harm in the church / Bridget Eileen Rivera.
Description: Grand Rapids, Michigan : Brazos Press, a division of Baker Publishing Group, [2021]
Identifiers: LCCN 2021018989 | ISBN 9781587434839 (paperback) | ISBN 9781587435393 (casebound) | ISBN 9781493432677 (ebook)
Subjects: LCSH: Christian sexual minorities—Religious life. | Church work with gays.
Classification: LCC BV4596.G38 R585 2021 | DDC 261.086/6—dc23
LC record available at https://lccn.loc.gov/2021018989

22   23   24   25   26   27   7   6   5   4

To the forgotten soul crying alone
in their bedroom with a Bible.
God loves you. **No matter what.**

Contents

9

BURDEN 6 Made in the Image of ~~God~~ Sex

BURDEN 7 Jesus ~~Saves~~ Damns

A Better Way

Introduction

For they preach, but do not practice. They tie up heavy burdens, hard to bear, and lay them on people's shoulders, but
they themselves are not willing to move them with their finger.

—Matthew 23:3–4

I squirmed in my seat, avoiding eye contact with the women
in my small group. They offered encouragement to a woman
sitting next to me. She spoke in halting sentences, wiping away
tears with a tissue they offered.

"It's just awful," she said. "You can't even imagine."

But I could.

She was talking about her son. Her gay son. And nobody
knew that he was gay but me and her. She didn't even know that
I knew. She didn't know that I knew he had a boyfriend. That
he had just come out to her a day ago. She didn't know that I
knew about it all.

She didn't know that I am gay too. None of them did.

"Pete just needs prayer," she said. "We learned some things
about him yesterday. I can't go into details, but he's falling
away."

I fingered the pages of my Bible nervously and found myself saying, "Your son loves Jesus. . . . He really does. God will watch out for him."

"This is just so terrible, Bridget," she said, eyes bleary and red. "I can't say what it is, but it's just so bad that I'd rather have learned he was dead."

I'd rather have learned he was dead.

Her words lingered in the air as I looked away. One of the ladies gave her hand a little squeeze, and the mother went on about her family's despair. A woman volunteered to pray for her. And then we moved on.

■ ■ ■

What is so bad about homosexuality that a Christian would rather a loved one be *dead* than gay? I've asked myself that question more times than I could count. Though her sentiment is shocking, the woman from my small group isn't an outlier. Her words reflect the secret and often unconscious thoughts of many Christians. Worse, her words reflect the silent voice of death whispering in the minds of countless LGBTQ people—people made in the image of God who often tragically believe they'd be better off dead than alive as they are.

The question is why?

Discrimination never starts with a death wish. It begins slowly. Imperceptibly. Lurking in a raised eyebrow and in the unspoken assumptions we make about normalcy. It flourishes in the hopes and dreams we nurture for ourselves and for our loved ones and in the prejudices we cultivate for those we despise. Until one day a parent wakes up and finds themself shedding more tears over their child being gay than being dead.

Until one day a child wakes up and actually *wants* to be dead.

■ ■ ■

Come to me, all who labor and are heavy laden, and I will give you rest. Take my yoke upon you, and learn from me, for I am gentle and lowly in heart, and you will find rest for your souls. For my yoke is easy, and my burden is light. (Matt. 11:28–30)

One of the greatest invitations of the gospel is an invitation to rest. Jesus not only brings life to his children. He brings a *good* life. Not a life without troubles, for sure, but one with troubles that are nevertheless *easy*. As he declared in the passage above, he brings a life with burdens that are *light*.

Objections abound to such a notion, even from Christians. What about taking up your cross to follow Jesus? Counting the cost? Dying to yourself and mortifying the flesh? Isn't the call to follow Jesus a call to share in his suffering?

And the answer is yes! But in our haste to emphasize the cost of following Jesus, we must not forget the blessing. According to Scripture, the burdens of Christ bring *peace* to our souls, not misery. "Take my yoke upon you," Jesus said, "and you will find *rest* for your souls."

Anyone who has ever done something good for the sake of doing something good knows what I'm talking about. There's a difference between giving your only slice of cake to your brother because you want to do something nice and your brother stealing that piece of cake. You "suffer" the loss of cake in both situations. But the first scenario makes you happy to see your brother enjoying your cake. The second just makes you angry.

Suffering for the sake of Christ is much the same. Christ calls each of us into a type of suffering that brings joy even in the midst of loss, a paradoxical burden that makes our journey easier, not harder. A mysteriously better way to enjoy our cake by giving it up. A way to live our life by losing it.

"The law of the LORD is perfect, reviving the soul," the psalmist declares. "The precepts of the LORD are right, rejoicing the heart" (Ps. 19:7a, 8a). If one thing is certain about

13

following Jesus, it's that following him is *good* for us. It revives us in the deserts of this world and makes our hearts "rejoice with joy that is inexpressible and filled with glory" (1 Pet. 1:8). The law of the Lord is "sweeter also than honey and drippings of the honeycomb" (Ps. 19:10) because it's not only objectively good but *subjectively* good too. It "tastes" good to follow God. His burdens feel light. In a world weighed down by sin, shame, and oppression, Jesus Christ delivers us from the weight of our present darkness.

It should come as no surprise, then, that Jesus pronounces anathema upon the religious leaders of his day, hypocrites who loaded the people of God with heavy burdens: "And [Jesus] said, 'Woe to you lawyers also! For you load people with burdens hard to bear, and you yourselves do not touch the burdens with one of your fingers. Woe to you!'" (Luke 11:46–47).

Indeed, heavy burdens pervert the very message of the gospel. Imagine walking with Christian in John Bunyan's *The Pilgrim's Progress*. You arrive at the cross, and Christian's burden slips from his back. But just as he's about to rejoice, a stranger suddenly appears with an even *greater* burden. He hoists it upon Christian's shoulders, replacing what Christ had taken away, and declares that Christian must journey all the way to the Celestial City like that. How far would Christian get?

The Problem

Countless LGBTQ believers find themselves struggling under the weight of burdens that no Christian should ever bear, burdens given to them not by Christ but by stigma, prejudice, and discrimination. They faithfully persevere in their journey to the Celestial City with a heroic degree of faithfulness, but they do so under the mounting pressure of an atmosphere hostile to their faith. What's worse, many sexual and gender minorities leave the faith altogether, their belief destroyed in the wake of abhorrent abuses that would test the resolve of the greatest of saints. Few Christians understand the extent of the problem, and even fewer are ready to acknowledge that Christian communities are responsible.

Indeed, discrimination against LGBTQ people exists at virtually every level of church involvement, from how sexual and gender minorities experience evangelism, to how they experience discipleship, community, accountability, ministry opportunities, counseling, mentorship, family, and friendship. More than one queer believer has told me that merely stepping over the threshold of a church causes their entire body to stiffen with fear. Others tell me that they no longer attend church at all because they've been rejected so many times; they can't bear to be rejected again.

It's a tragedy experienced by millions of LGBTQ people who grew up in the church, have attempted to join the church, or have encountered the church in some way during their lifetime. A tragedy measured in the silent tears they shed and ultimately counted in the bodies of the many LGBTQ people who die by suicide every year.

Lesbian, gay, and bisexual youth contemplate suicide three times more often than heterosexual youth and are 8.4 times more likely to attempt suicide if they experience family rejection.[1] Forty percent of transgender adults have attempted suicide at least once in their lifetime, and of that number, 92 percent attempted suicide before the age of twenty-five.[2] Of all teen suicides from 2013 to 2015, nearly 25 percent were LGBTQ.[3] Of all homeless youth in the United States, 40 percent are LGBTQ.[4] In the span of a year, an estimated 1.8 million LGBTQ youth between the ages of thirteen and twenty-four will seriously contemplate suicide.[5] LGBTQ people are also more likely to be the target of hate crimes than any other minority group in the United States today, surpassing Jewish, Muslim, and Black people.[6]

For most people, religious involvement reduces the risk of suicide. But when gay and lesbian college students engage more heavily in their faith communities, their risk of suicide only goes up.[7] Gay and lesbian students are 38 percent more likely to contemplate suicide if they are heavily involved in faith communities. Lesbian students, counted separately from gay male students, are 52 percent more likely to contemplate suicide if they are heavily involved in faith communities.[8] How can that be? How is it that going to church would be a factor in keeping straight people alive but pushing gay people toward death?

The discrimination facing LGBTQ people in the church is no secret. The vast majority of non-Christians in the United States (as much as 91 percent) believe Christians to be homophobic.[9] Consider these observations from two leading researchers who are Christians themselves: "Outsiders say our hostility toward gays—not just opposition to homosexual politics and behaviors but disdain for gay individuals—has become virtually synonymous with the Christian faith. . . . When you introduce yourself as a Christian to a friend, neighbor, or business associate who is an outsider, you might as well have it tattooed on your arm: antihomosexual, gay-hater, homophobic. I doubt you think of yourself in these terms, but that's what outsiders think of you."[10]

A Better Church

A queer friend of mine once likened her experience in the church to standing in a field in a thunderstorm. Every drop of rain is a new slight, another put-down, another reminder that you're the wrong kind of person. Talking about it can feel like trying to talk about the wetness of a single drop of rain. *What's the big deal?* people say. But it's not a particular raindrop that causes the problem. The problem is the storm. Some people get pushed by the wind, others get stuck in the mud, and a few get struck by lightning. But *everybody* is scared and cold and wet.

Tragically, many LGBTQ Christians find their church to be the source of the storm when it ought to be the shelter. They first experience marginalization in the context of church, they find Christians to be the most common perpetrators of prejudice against them, and they learn to avoid everything to do with Christianity as a means of sheer survival.

It should not be this way.

In the following pages, I explore how we got here, the impact on LGBTQ people, and what it might look like to chart a better path forward. Unlike most books that tackle LGBTQ issues in Christianity, this book is not going to spend much time debating whether same-sex marriage is biblical. Instead, I will unpack the consequences of LGBTQ discrimination *regardless* of your theological position in the "big debate."

I myself am a lesbian who follows what's known as the "traditional" sexual ethic. This means that I've chosen celibacy as a vocation instead of marriage, and that I'm invested in discovering pathways within celibacy that are healthy and life-giving. However, if I've found one thing to be true when it comes to LGBTQ issues in the church, it's that many of us get so caught up on gay marriage that we forget there's more at stake.

Countless LGBTQ people grow up in churches believing that God hates them—the climax to a story that we've told ourselves about sex and gender that elevates cisgender heterosexuality as the only valid human experience and that labels all other experiences sinful. We're going to unpack that story together. More than that, we're going to shift our focus away from LGBTQ issues as the source of our problems and, instead, look at the church itself. Self-examination is hard, but that's what this book is about. I'll be asking us to put a magnifying lens to the church, and together, we'll consider how *Christians* have contributed to lasting trauma for LGBTQ people, many of whom are siblings in Christ.

Tackling this topic is no easy endeavor. Nearly everything I address in the following pages deserves its own volume. If

I covered everything, I imagine I'd be writing for a lifetime. Instead, my goal is to explore a *few* key issues that impact everything about how LGBTQ people experience the church, extending so far as to shape the very way that LGBTQ Christians think about themselves and culminating in the suicide of thousands—a totalizing system that many find impossible to escape.

For every story you read in the following pages, countless more exist just like it. I invite you to grapple with these stories and to unpack their causes and, moreover, to consider what this means for the church moving forward. The people of God represent the hands and feet of Christ to a broken world, bringing God's healing touch to you and to me and to every person we meet. As the body of Christ, we incarnate the goodness of the gospel. We represent a life-giving Savior who doesn't rest with ninety-nine sheep out of a hundred. He goes out, and he searches, and he rescues, saving the smallest and most insignificant member of his flock. He isn't happy with saving "most" of the flock. He works until every last one of his sheep experiences the love and care and mercy of his fold (Matt. 18:10–14).

The heart of Jesus breaks with every broken heart, and he mourns the mistreatment of every vulnerable soul. A day will come when he will look upon each of us, and he won't ask us about our ninety-nine friends. He'll ask us about the one, and he'll want to know how we treated the one; and on that day, he will declare, "As you did it to one of the least of these my brothers, you did it to me" (Matt. 25:40).

LGBTQ people are the "one." But how exactly have Christians treated them? What is it like to be queer in the church? Why is it like that, and how can we change? If you genuinely want to know, this book is for you.

BURDEN 1

SEX ...
ERR ...
CELIBACY
IS GREAT!

1. The Protestant Sexual Revolution

STEPHEN

Growing up in a conservative, evangelical context, Stephen learned that gay sex was an abomination. If he messed up now and again, it might not be the end of the world, as long as he repented. But with eternal damnation ever looming in the background, he could never be sure if he had repented enough.

"My theology was a form of slow suicide," Stephen recalled. "It didn't matter how hard I tried, and it didn't matter how many things I did right, it still tortured me." He found himself spiraling in and out of anguish and suicidal thoughts, his sexuality consuming his life. "It was like this cut in my mouth that I just couldn't stop feeling. Even on good days, it was still there eating away at me. I lost a good portion of my life to it."

Stephen dropped out of high school. Though he eventually returned to complete his education and enrolled in college classes, he failed multiple courses each semester and took eight years to finally graduate. Over time, he developed a network of Christian friends who were okay with him as long as he was celibate. But he didn't know if he could honestly be celibate for the rest of his life.

Friends suggested he look to Henri Nouwen, a "hero of gay celibacy," for inspiration. One article in particular described Nouwen as "choosing to live the wound," as Stephen put it. "Again and again and again," Stephen recalled, "he just chose to embrace and live the wound." Stephen was in his early twenties at the time, and the article filled him with despair.

"I'm looking at the rest of my life, and this is what I'm being told is the best that I can look forward to. It just destroyed me. It just crushed me." But he couldn't budge on gay celibacy because "to do so would be to live in mortal error." It was grin and bear it or go to hell. But he found himself getting to the point where he didn't know if he could bear it any longer.

"I thought, 'I might as well just kill myself now. If this is all I have to look forward to in life, I don't think I can do it.'"

■ ■ ■

During the early years of the culture wars in twentieth-century America, a kind of righteous fervor gripped the faithful in countless evangelical churches. Christian leaders cast their followers as valiant soldiers in a grandiose battle for the soul of their country, a struggle in which sex, marriage, and the nuclear family took center stage. Sexual liberation threatened the very fabric of society. Fornication, adultery, serial monogamy, divorce, abortion, pregnancy out of wedlock, homosexuality—all of it loomed large in the evangelical imagination. Sexual autonomy threatened the building blocks of Western civilization. Apart from drastic Christian action, society itself would crumble.[1]

Among the most prominent theologians of this era was Carl F. H. Henry, who published a scathing indictment of American liberalism titled *Twilight of a Great Civilization*. Writing in the late 1980s, he argued that shifting norms of immorality and "sexual libertinism"[2] in particular sounded the death knells of not only the United States but ultimately Western culture. Describing a showdown of cosmic proportions, he called for Christians to band together against the forces of secular humanism, political leftism, and sexual liberation "before hell breaks out."[3] "A half-generation ago the pagans were still largely threatening at the gates of Western culture," he said. "Now the barbarians are plunging into the oriental and occidental mainstream."[4]

As a result of this "barbarian" invasion, Christians had no choice but to fight back. Henry enlisted imagery from Sodom and Gomorrah to summarize his battle cry, calling on Christians of every stripe to "wake up" before the sun sets: "When that great meltdown comes, where will you be? Trapped in Sodom? In the bleak twilight of a decadent culture, where will you be? Overtaken, like Lot, looking back at the citadels of sin? 'Wake up!' says Paul; 'wake up!' American culture is sinking toward sunset."[5]

By linking our dystopian future of "sexual libertinism" to the forces of radical leftism, secular humanism, and the "gay agenda," evangelical leaders created a moral panic in the Christian imagination. *We* faithful Christians stood as the vanguards of biblical morality against *them*, the leftist agents and sexual deviants who will destroy the nuclear family and civilization as we know it. "We're living in the outpouring of the wrath of God in the category of His abandoning a culture," John MacArthur said in 2012, "and we're living in the sequence that is here: a sexual revolution, a homosexual revolution, a reprobate mind that unleashes everything, including murder on a massive scale and hate toward God."[6]

But a deep irony lies at the bottom of this panic. Despite decades of rhetoric blaming the "secular left" for the explosion of sexual liberation in the twentieth century, the basic ideology behind sexual autonomy didn't originate in leftist propaganda. It didn't begin with the gay agenda or even the sexual revolution of the 1960s. It began with a movement far deeper in the history of Western civilization—a sexual revolution with far greater consequences than anything accomplished in the 1960s. One that continues to shape how we think about sexuality and,

ultimately, what we believe to be true about the most fundamental aspects of human identity.

It was the Protestant Reformation. And it changed everything.

A History of the Revolution

Martin Luther exploded onto the scene of Western Christianity
with a radical new idea that would alter the course of history:
Sex is a necessary good. Sex is "not a matter of choice or decision but a natural and necessary thing," Martin Luther said.
"It is just as necessary as the fact that I am a man, and more
necessary than sleeping and waking, eating and drinking, and
emptying the bowels and bladder." He argued for an understanding of not just human sexuality but sex itself as "innate"
to human existence.[7]

Luther's message stood in contrast to the prevailing beliefs
about human sexuality at the time. Catholic doctrine about sex
and marriage had dominated the religious landscape for over a
millennium, teaching that holiness required a renunciation of
sexual desire, even in the context of marriage. Chastity, particularly celibate virginity, was the ideal. Marriage was a lesser
calling for those too weak to abstain. Anyone who carried a
position of spiritual authority was expected to be celibate,
and church governance regulated all aspects of married life
in an effort to limit sexual expression to procreative purposes
alone.

Medieval historian James Brundage describes the situation in
his book *Law, Sex, and Christian Society in Medieval Europe.*
Even marital intercourse was "always impure, and always sinful"[8] unless accomplished without the faintest hint of sexual
desire, a requirement difficult to fathom. Sex came to be seen
in Christian teaching as the vehicle through which original
sin passed from parent to child—a fundamental expression
of human depravity, necessary only for procreation. Chastity

24

in marriage became nearly impossible, as any hint of sexual desire betrayed sinful motivations.

The resulting ascetic atmosphere cast human sexuality itself as the root of all evil, the cause of original sin, and the reason why every last man, woman, and child was tainted by iniquity. Penitential writers developed such a complex web of limitations on marital sexual activity that it became difficult to discern just *when* sex was permissible, if ever. Pious couples who attempted to observe the prohibitions, says Brundage, "would have found the process of deciding whether or not they could in good conscience have intercourse at any given moment a complex, perhaps even frightening, process."[9]

Not surprisingly, mandated celibacy was a natural requirement for the priesthood. Celibacy was the *only* surefire way to pursue true and lasting holiness. By the time of the Reformation, this approach to human sexuality had become so institutionalized within Christian teaching that few could imagine the Bible teaching otherwise.

Until Luther.

Undergirding Luther's rejection of clerical celibacy was a rejection of the idea that human sexuality was inherently sinful. It was tainted by sin, Luther argued, just as all aspects of humanity are, but sexuality was a good thing created by God nevertheless. In one sermon, Luther humorously observed that even eating and drinking are tainted by sin, but eating and drinking are no more inherently evil than anything else innate to the human condition, including when people "purge themselves and pick and blow their noses."[10] He continued, "Why do you only look at the impurity that exists in marriage? If you want to talk about the kind of purity and chastity that the angels have, you will find it nowhere, neither in marriage nor out of it in the unmarried condition. Purity does not exist; even children are not pure."[11]

Having rejected the medieval Catholic belief that human sexuality is inherently evil, Luther argued that celibacy is a "special gift" that few possess.[12] "It is a devilish tyranny to require it."[13] "This is a matter of nature and not of choice."[14] Celibacy was not just unreasonable but an affront to human nature. "No one is bound to obey such a command, and the pope is responsible for all the sins that are committed against it."[15]

Not surprisingly, as the Reformation spread throughout Europe, sex-positive discourse began to proliferate. For the first time in centuries, not only could clergymen get married; they could also talk about sex! Prominent clergymen, such as William Gouge, told married Christians to yield "that due benevolence [sex] one to another which is warranted and sanctified by God's Word."[16] Sexual intercourse, he said, was a "domesticall dutie" that God had ordained for the good of his people. Many likened intercourse to a spiritual experience.[17] Others urged their congregants to actually *enjoy* sex.[18]

Marriage had always been seen as a picture of Christ and the church, but Protestants began to locate within sex itself a means of receiving God's grace. Theologian Richard Sibbes, in a sermon called "Bowels Opened," used overtly sexual language to describe Jesus in shockingly erotic terms, beckoning his congregants to "open, open still" that Christ might "come into us."[19]

Even theologians who resisted the Reformation began to shift their beliefs about sex. Erasmus, for example, who had attempted an air of neutrality toward the Reformation, nevertheless agreed with the reformers that sex is "fair and holy." Why would God give us "these pricks and provocations"? he reasoned, referring to sexual desire. God makes nothing in vain, he continued, so why make us sexual if not to have sex? "Virginity is a divine thing," Erasmus concluded. "But wedlock is a human thing."[20]

Bending the Rules and Redefining Marriage

The consequences of reframing sex as a necessary good meant that marriage could no longer be understood as it had been for centuries. Martin Luther and John Calvin argued medieval Catholicism elevated marriage as a sacrament in service to its lust for power. Because the Catholic Church reserved the right to regulate everything about the sacraments, marriage had become an extension of religious authoritarianism, leading to greater sexual sin, not less.[21] "It may truly be affirmed," Calvin argued, "that, when they made matrimony into a sacrament, they only sought a den of all abominations."[22] "Not only is marriage regarded as a sacrament without the least warrant of Scripture," Luther said in *Babylonian Captivity* (written in 1520), "but the very ordinances that extol it as a sacrament have turned it into a farce."[23] Undergirded by Luther's conception of the two kingdoms, reformers located marriage within the domain of earthly affairs, redefining it as a "worldly"institution that existed in the kingdom of earth as opposed to the kingdom of heaven.[24] It was a covenant before God (as Calvin articulated) but certainly not a sacrament.

Luther went so far as to advise leaders to follow local customs governing marriage: "Every land has its own customs, according to the common saying. In keeping with this, because weddings and marriages are the business of the world, it is not proper for us clergymen or servants of the church to arrange or govern them. On the contrary, let each city and land follow its own usage and custom, however they go."[25] In later writings, Luther maintained a strict separation between the temporal and spiritual realms, arguing that "marriage is an external, worldly matter, like clothing and food, house and property, subject to temporal authority, as the many imperial laws enacted on the subject prove."[26]

But isn't marriage an ordinance of God? the naysayers countered. Well, sure it is, said the reformers. But so is agriculture; should we make agriculture a sacrament?[27] *But marriage represents Christ and the church, the very kingdom of heaven!* Sure it does, said the Protestants. But so does a mustard seed; should we make mustard-seed planting a sacrament too?[28] "Upon this principle, everything will be a sacrament," Calvin remarked, tongue-in-cheek.[29]

To be clear, reformers were *not* trying to overthrow marriage as a thing of moral consequence. They believed that marriage carried a great deal of ethical and theological weight; Calvin taught that marriage represented a solemn, lifelong covenant before God. Even though Protestants fought for local determination in regulating marriage, no one would have tried to argue that marriage was merely a social construct. Instead, they opposed the authoritarian system in Roman Catholicism that prevented everyday people from getting married—despite the approval of friends, family, and neighbors. Even more, they argued that mandated celibacy led to rampant sexual immorality.

These were the issues at the forefront of people's minds that reformers were trying to fix. Divorce was still a grave sin, and procreation was still understood to be the purpose of sexual intercourse. Though Luther rejected the idea that intercourse itself was the vehicle through which original sin passed from parent to child, he still recognized that all things, including human sexuality, were infected by original sin.[30] Notably, he even believed that adulterers should be put to death, though he thought the government should do it, not the church.[31]

Nevertheless, in deconstructing the Catholic Church's control over the institution of marriage, Protestants gifted the Western world with a new way of thinking about human sexuality. With the exception that priests could now marry, not much looked different on the outside, especially to a present-day observer. However, tectonic shifts had nevertheless taken place in the assumptions underneath people's behavior. These shifts would now form the basis of a new sexual order.

2. The New Sexual Order

CHANG

Chang's youth group talked about sex all the time. But not how most people would imagine. Teens out in the world talked about sex because they couldn't keep their hands off each other. But Christian teens talked about sex because God made sex, and it was *good*. At least, that's how Chang's church explained it. All they had to do was wait to get married, and God would bless them with a wonderful sex life.

Chang heard sermon after sermon about waiting for marriage, learned how to "stay vertical" when spending time with a guy, and internalized important principles, like never being alone with the opposite sex. But sex itself wasn't bad. Rather, sex was *so* good that you had to make sure you didn't ruin it. Her church hosted a "Silver Ring Thing" event, where Chang's friends lined up to pay twenty dollars each for a silver ring that signified their commitment to purity. The best kind of sex would come to those who waited for it.

Chang never fully internalized the "sex is great" rhetoric of her white evangelical church, even though it surrounded her. Something about it seemed off. Why did they have to talk about sex so much in the first place? "I was like, Can't we talk about something else? Like God?" she recalled.

And then she discovered that she was bisexual. Nothing in her Christian sex education had prepared her for that discovery. In college, she talked frequently with mentors and wrestled with Scripture. But the more she wrestled, the more questions she had. The more she wondered whether same-sex marriage could be biblical.

That scared Chang. That kind of thinking was dangerous. It could easily get her kicked out of her campus ministry. Her Christian social circle encompassed her entire life. She couldn't lose that.

She prayed that God would confirm that same-sex relationships were wrong. But a miracle never came. She dated a girl for a few weeks hoping that God would expose how terrible it was. Nothing serious, just a few dates. But God never did.

Until then, Chang had been afraid to tell the campus ministry leader, who had been mentoring her, that she might be questioning her beliefs about same-sex marriage. It seemed like a line she couldn't cross, but she realized she needed to talk. She finally called him at the end of the semester, and they met for coffee.

"I thought you were smarter than this," he said. "You should know better."

He told her to step down from the leadership team, preventing her from leading Bible studies or even volunteering with the soundboard crew. "It was like the idea that questioning this one thing that we had all agreed on threatened everything."

She had straight friends volunteering in the ministry with more lenient views about sex and marriage than she did. Why didn't they get kicked out of volunteer work? What was so dangerous about the questions she had? Why couldn't she ask and look for answers like anybody else?

■ ■ ■

The consequences of removing marriage from the sacraments are so vast that it's doubtful the reformers grasped the full ramifications. But they certainly understood the immediate benefits. "Restore freedom to everybody," Luther proclaimed. "Leave every man the free choice to marry or not to marry."[1] Let the saint and the zealot be celibate if they choose, but "why should another's holiness disturb my liberty? . . . Let him not rob me of my liberty!"[2]

Marriage thus became a human right, one that religious authority had no business controlling and which could not be denied without restricting basic liberties.

Undergirding this transformation was a shift in Christians' assumptions about sex. Previously, facts about human biology—specifically sex and sexual desire—had been seen as largely inconsequential to Christian ideas about marriage. Marriage itself had governed the Christian approach to sex, and desire, in turn, had little to do with defining the boundaries of morality.

The reformers upended this schema.

"Why should people marry," Luther mused, "unless they have desire and love for another?"[3] Sex is "a matter of nature and not of choice." Denying people the right to marry, he reasoned, compels them to sin. "You may be sure," he wrote in *The Estate of Marriage*, "that they will not remain pure but inevitably besmirch themselves with secret sins or fornication. For they are incapable of resisting the word and ordinance of God within them."[4]

At one point, Luther suggested that if a woman were married to an "impotent" man and "burned with desire" on account of his impotence, he would counsel her to "contract a marriage to another and flee to a distant unknown place."[5] When Catholics responded with outrage, he explained that he wouldn't actually counsel her to flee. He would merely encourage her to discuss the matter with her husband and, after gaining his consent, get married to another man in secret.[6]

Luther was speaking hypothetically, but his musings reveal how far things had shifted. Historian Steven Ozment summarizes the consequences: "The Protestant reformers tolerated . . . for the first time in the West on Christian grounds, genuine divorce and remarriage. Although they viewed marriage as a spiritual bond transcending all other human relationships, marriage was not a church sacrament that created a once-and-for-all state; a marriage could definitely end this side of eternity and a new one begin for separated spouses."[7] Forcing unhappy couples to stay married no longer made sense. More than that, in a world where sexual frustration leads to sin, requiring divorcees to be celibate looked no better than requiring priests to be celibate.

Although most of the early reformers explicitly connected sex to procreation, discussion of procreation became less and less central as Protestant reformers increasingly adopted a narrative about marriage that prioritized sexual and romantic fulfillment. Well-known clergymen and theologians talked more and more about marriage in terms of "fellowship," "companionship," "love," "joy," "copartnership," "conjugal affection," "mutual delight," and "heaven on earth."[8] This language shifted the focus away from procreation and toward a conception of love that buoyed the development of romance in the eighteenth century.[9]

Naturally, if sexual pleasure is a good thing in itself, it's not too far a jump to conclude that sexual intercourse is permissible outside of procreation. In the nineteenth and twentieth centuries, contraception evolved into an acceptable point of disagreement among Christians until it eventually became majority practice. By the early to mid-twentieth century, Protestant denominations were lobbying *en masse* to legalize contraception.[10] Today, 93 percent of Protestants and 89 percent of Catholics believe that contraception is either morally acceptable or morally neutral.[11]

Taken altogether, Reformation ideas altered the logic by which sex and marriage were understood, allowing Christians to explore possibilities that would have been unthinkable a century before. Things didn't change overnight. Divorce was still discouraged, procreation still very *en*couraged, and anything related to same-sex intercourse still considered an abomination. Nevertheless, the reformers introduced new assumptions

32

to the Christian imagination—sex and sexuality as integral to human identity; celibacy as unnatural; marriage as a human right; pursuit of marriage for romantic love. All these ideas remain embedded within the legacy of Protestant teaching. It wasn't the 1960s that bequeathed such ideas to Western society. And it wasn't gay people either. It was the Reformation and the Christians who helmed it.

The Ongoing Legacy

The legacy of sexual liberation in modern Christianity exposes a reality at the heart of contemporary debates over sex and marriage: both conservative evangelicals *and* their liberal counterparts in mainline denominations owe their existence to a movement deeply committed to redefining Christian sexual morality. Sex, marriage, and human sexuality have always been contested ideas in Protestant denominations, and Protestants have long accommodated sticky ethical dilemmas when it comes to these topics, leading to a broad acceptance of divorce, remarriage, and contraception despite the historic understanding of Scripture.

The end result is a system that would have been alien to most people at the start of the Reformation but that is largely taken for granted by many Christians today. What Christians today might call "biblical teaching on marriage and sexuality"— whereby two people of the opposite sex pursue sexual fulfillment in the context of a romantic marriage relationship—is actually quite modern.

Even more, many Christians now take for granted that lifelong celibacy is impossible. Albert Mohler, President of Southern Baptist Theological Seminary, teaches that it is "unreasonable for [people] to refrain from sex"[12] and that choosing singleness when you experience sexual desire is a "neglect of Christian responsibility."[13] Prominent theologian John MacArthur likewise teaches that "there's a place for voluntary celibacy. It's a blessing if you have the gift, as Paul put it. But to deny someone normal family life, to deny someone normal relationships, is a cruel, cruel thing." He further argues that forcing people to be celibate leads to "sexual perversion."[14] The implication is that people *need* sex to live a healthy life.

Such logic inevitably places sexual fulfillment (as opposed to procreation) at the center of the marriage relationship. Consider the following excerpt from Ray Ortlund's *Marriage and the Mystery of the Gospel*, where he speaks to the problem of lust: "Wisdom is *not* saying, 'You feel desire? And there's temptation out there? Then what you need is an iron will. So there's your future—endless frustration bottled up inside.' Self-control is an important part of maturity. But wisdom believes that God's remedy for a man's thirst for sex is sex—an overflowing sexual joy with his wife: 'your own cistern,' 'your own well.' A man's wife is his own personal, divinely approved wellspring of endless sexual satisfaction."[15]

The notion that "God's remedy for sex is sex" reflects a reimagining of sexual desire wherein sex is the only way to "satisfy" our sexuality. Classically, Christians understood sexuality as a thing to be stewarded. "Satisfaction" was not the point so much as faithfulness, whether in celibacy or marriage. Ortlund's focus on "joyously bubbling sexual happiness between husband and wife" as being the "remedy" for desire effectively situates sex at the center of not only marriage but human fulfillment. The implication is that a man is doomed, apart from marriage, to "endless frustration bottled up inside."[16]

It's no coincidence that Christian sex manuals have exploded in the past century, from Tim and Beverly LaHaye's *The Act of Marriage: The Beauty of Sexual Love*, which contains illustrations and sexual techniques, to Mark and Grace Driscoll's *Real Marriage: The Truth about Sex, Friendship, and Life Together*, where married Christians learn about their biblical freedom to engage in masturbation, oral sex, anal sex, menstrual sex, and cybersex. Far from being a departure from "stuffy" Christian teaching, such writing typifies the prurient ethic of Protestantism. Scholar Amy DeRogatis summarizes it well: "The main message of evangelical sex manuals is that frequent and mutually satisfying sexual encounters are crucial for a strong marriage. Sex is sanctioned by God, should be practiced in marriage, and is one of the wonders of creation. In most cases, the writers downplay reproduction and focus on mutual sexual pleasure as the fulfillment of God's plan for humanity. . . . Evangelical sex manuals allow the faithful to participate in an American culture that they often describe as 'over-sexualized' while still affirming biblical principles."[17]

A striking example of this phenomenon is purity culture, an evangelical subculture intended to combat sexual immorality that largely depends on beliefs mirroring those of sexual progressivism—just as long as you wait for God to give you a heterosexual marriage. Conferences in the '90s and 2000s, like the Silver Ring Thing, sold T-shirts reading, "How to Have the Best Sex Ever,"[18] and featured attractive twenty-somethings on stage leading teens to chant, "Sex is great! Sex is great!" before concluding, "and it is great, in the context of marriage."[19] Jim Burns's *Purity Code* includes detailed descriptions of male and female anatomy and promises adolescent readers that following the "purity code" will bring them "freedom and set [their] future up for joy."[20] Dannah Gresh uses a similar line of reasoning in *And the Bride Wore White: Seven Secrets to Sexual Purity*. She describes a couple who remained virgins until their wedding day and says, "*I am pretty sure that Jenny and Bryan have glorious sex, and I believe it is because God has blessed their marriage covenant.* I truly believe that when we keep that covenant by saving ourselves to love someone with all the intensity of our heart and body, He is able to bless us immeasurably beyond what we could have imagined within our sex lives."[21]

The message is clear: follow God's rules, and he'll bless you with an incredible sex life through marriage. "If we gladly obey all that God has said about sex, within the promises of a covenant before God," said Marshall Segal, writing for Desiring God in 2019, "he gives sex a depth the world has never known."[22] Sex, write the LaHayes, is the "most thrilling, exciting, and fulfilling experience in the world."[23] Writing for Focus on the Family, Rob Jackson says that "our earthly expressions of sexuality in marriage are the closest approximation to the unity, joy, and pleasurable fulfillment we will experience in heaven."[24]

The result is a worldview, evolved over the past five hundred years, that promises heterosexual Christians everything they could possibly desire out of sex, as long as it takes place within the context of heterosexual marriage. Marriage can be defined apart from the sacraments. It can be defined apart from procreation. It can even be defined apart from a lifelong, one-flesh union, as even remarriage is okay.

But it *can't* be defined apart from the sexual needs and desires of everyday Christians who happen to be straight.

Sexual Liberation with a Christian Twist

This leads to an uncomfortable truth: Protestant Christianity is a Christianity that is deeply in love with sex. Although many conservative evangelicals commonly view sexual liberation as contradicting their beliefs, the sexual revolution of the twentieth century, far from being a rebellion against Christianity, was in fact a very natural evolution of the basic premises developed by Christians five hundred years prior.

The biggest difference, of course, is the belief that sex is reserved for marriage between a man and a woman. But because Protestant Christianity shares the same narrative about human sexuality as liberalism, Protestant beliefs about sex and marriage ultimately reflect the same worldview. Consider the following arguments side by side:

> [Sex] is just as necessary as the fact that I am a man, and more necessary than sleeping and waking, eating and drinking, and emptying the bowels and bladder. It is a nature and disposition just as innate as the organs involved in it. (Martin Luther)[25]

> If it have been rightly everywhere pronounced as a proverb, that God nor nature have made no thing frustrate nor in vain, why (I pray you) hath God given us these members? Why these pricks and provocations? . . . Moreover, in other beasts, I pray you from whence cometh those pricks and provocations? Of nature, or of sin? Wonder it is if not of nature. . . . Surely we make that by our imagination to be foul, which of the self nature is fair and holy. (Erasmus)[26]

> It's better to marry than to—what?—than to burn. It's better to marry than burn with passion. And certainly 1 Corinthians 7 makes it very clear that singleness is not preferable to marriage. To make celibacy mandatory is utterly unbiblical. (John MacArthur)[27]

> I am suggesting that when people wait until their mid-to-late 20s to marry, it is unreasonable to expect them to refrain from sex. (Al Mohler)[28]

> Christians throughout history have affirmed that lifelong celibacy is a spiritual gift and calling, not a path that should be forced upon someone. Yes, permanently forgoing marriage is a worthy choice for Christians who are gifted with celibacy. But it must be a choice. (Matthew Vines)[29]

All of these authors are Christians, and all of them make similar arguments about celibacy. But only one of them would be considered unchristian or unbiblical. Matthew Vines, coincidentally, is gay. The Christian tradition that tells people that celibacy is "cruel,"[30] that the answer to their sexual frustration is having sex,[31] and that sex through marriage is the "most fulfilling experience in the world"[32] also tells gay people to marry a person they don't find attractive or else be celibate forever. The result is a system that excludes people from understanding their sexuality in any meaningful way unless they experience attraction to the opposite sex and only the opposite sex.

Chang, whose story I shared earlier, spent her teenage years attending conferences where they chanted "Sex is great!" and youth groups where the leaders bragged about their hot wives and great sex lives. At her college, her campus ministry permitted a host of perspectives and convictions about marriage, and she noted that most of the ministry's straight participants had more lenient ideas about sex than she did. None of them faced reprisal for their perspectives. It was only Chang who was punished, and it was only after she started questioning her beliefs about same-sex marriage.

Stephen's story, which I shared at the beginning of chapter 1, also echoes the double standard. As a gay man, he felt forced into celibacy, and Christians told him to look to historical celibate figures (such as Henri Nouwen) for inspiration. However, Christians also talked about such people as being miserable. And Stephen *was* miserable.

It's not lost on gay people that few straight Christians learn that suffering is the point of sexual ethics. In fact, they learn the opposite: "If we gladly obey all that God has said about sex, within the promises of a covenant before God, he gives sex a depth the world has never known."[33] But Stephen learned that Christian obedience was a "wound" that he must live "again and again."

Both Chang's and Stephen's experiences highlight the ways in which many evangelical Christians promote a narrative about human sexuality that contradicts the expectations placed on queer people. The message that LGBTQ people internalize is that God promises wonderful things in exchange for Christian obedience—but only if you're straight.

BURDEN I SUMMARY

We thus conclude the first burden that LGBTQ people bear in the church. Many straight Christians tell gay people to be celibate forever even as their own tradition has evolved to eliminate any similar requirement for themselves. Lifelong celibacy is possible, they say. But most don't believe it. Most only say so when talking to gay people.

BURDEN 2

SINNERS ~~SAVED BY~~ ~~GRACE~~

3. Perverted Identity

VICTOR

Victor grew up going to church multiple times a week. His dad led Bible studies, and his mom taught at the Christian school he attended. He went to sexual purity campaigns like the True Love Waits conference and bought a silver ring to symbolize his commitment to purity.

Victor was also attracted to men. Around age eleven, he started viewing gay porn. When his parents found out, they sent him to several biblical counselors. One after the other, they attempted to get rid of his same-sex attraction. The goal was to discover, in Victor's words, "Why do I feel this and how do I not feel this?" The message was, "I'm different and I shouldn't be different, and I really need to try to *not* be different."

A deacon reached out to Victor. He was also a teacher at the Christian middle school where Victor was attending, and he was highly respected in their community. In many ways, he represented the type of man Victor was trying to be: married with lovely children and a faithful ministry. At age twelve, Victor trusted him. Exploiting Victor's youth and relative ignorance, the man lured Victor into a sexually abusive relationship in which he molested Victor for three years.

When the truth about the abuse came out, the police opened an investigation and arrested the man. However, many in Victor's church responded to the investigation with hostility. "People blamed me," Victor said. "I felt like I was at fault."

Victor's church knew that he was gay, and they knew that he was in counseling for it. "We don't know the whole story," some speculated, as he recalled. "The boy doesn't seem innocent." Quickly, the narrative spread that Victor must have done something to seduce the man.

"He was just such a respected person," Victor said. "People liked him, and he was super nice. They just had a hard time attributing this really horrendous action to a man that represented something different."

On one side, there was a man of God who could do no wrong, who represented everything that a Christian man should be. On the other side was a young gay boy who couldn't stop looking at porn.

"I guess it *is* my fault," Victor concluded at the time. "Because of my sexuality, I can't be trusted."

■ ■ ■

When the Protestant reformers called for doing away with clerical celibacy, they defended their position by tying sexual desire to human nature. You might remember Luther saying that sexual intercourse is "just as necessary as the fact that I am a man."[1] Consider his words in context, from *The Estate of Marriage*:

> For this word which God speaks, "Be fruitful and multiply," is not a command. It is *more* than a command, namely, a divine ordinance which it is not our prerogative to hinder or ignore. Rather, it is just as necessary as the fact that I am a man, and more necessary than sleeping and waking, eating and drinking, and emptying the bowels and bladder. It is a *nature and disposition* just as *innate* as the organs involved in it. Therefore, just as God does not command anyone to be a man or a woman but creates them *the way they have to be*, so He does not command them to multiply but *creates them so that they have to* multiply.[2]

Here, we see an early Christian rationale for sexuality as something deeper than just the "organs involved in it," as a "nature and disposition" that is "innate," built into the most constitutive elements of our being. No longer was sexual desire a mere biological reality. It was embedded into the nature of what it meant to be a man or a woman, shaping our most innate dispositions and personality. We don't act sexual. We *are* sexual.

Such thinking contributed to a newly developing anthropology wherein sex was essentialized, meaning sex was increasingly seen as a defining part of the "essence" of human nature. Concepts of normalcy in sexual behavior soon attached themselves to concepts of normalcy in human *identity*. Heterosexuality didn't have a name yet, but a framework for thinking about it slowly evolved as ideas about the sexual purity of the "white" race—compared to the perversion of Indigenous and African "savages"—gradually emerged.[3]

It began with racial justifications for "New World" conquest, slavery, and empire. Writers described African men and women as sexually voracious and animalistic. Stories of sodomites from exotic lands sprinkled the accounts of explorers and travelers. Military generals portrayed Indigenous tribes as overrun by "effeminates." A "geography of perversion" gained popularity in the West, wherein white Europeans theorized that tropical climates produce sexual perversion. "Perversion" became one way (among many) that white colonizers could distinguish themselves from so-called inferior races.[4]

However, differences between the races proved insufficient to explain immoral behavior in white communities. To address this, scientists posited that sexual perversion represented a kind of vestigial reminder of less advanced periods in human history. It was "endemic" to Black and Indigenous communities. In white communities, it was a type of regression.[5]

Underneath such theories was a more fundamental innovation: discourse had evolved from "perversion" *as an act* to "the pervert" *as an individual*. By the late 1800s, sexologists and psychopathologists were building theories to explain the existence of "sodomites." Notable among them was Richard von Krafft-Ebing. Building on the work of German theorists, Krafft-Ebing introduced the words *homosexual*, *heterosexual*, and *bisexual* to the English language. His major work, *Psychopathia Sexualis*, presupposed the existence of two classes of individuals: "tainted" and "untainted."[6] Tainted individuals succumb to "manifestations of degeneration," while untainted individuals remain immune to such "inversions."[7] His book-length study of sexual perversion posited that homosexuality was a "neuropathic taint" and a "functional sign of degeneration."[8]

It was the first major English-language analysis of homosexuality, and it cemented sexual "class" as a structural method for studying perversion. Freud followed Krafft-Ebing and defined homosexuality as a psychopathological disorder.

Freud's writing centered on the story of Oedipus Rex, the Greek myth in which Oedipus unwittingly kills his father and marries his mother. Freud believed that the "Oedipus Complex" plays a central role in the human psyche.[9] Young boys develop in competition to their father for their mother's affection. Resolving this tension depends on the boy eventually identifying with the father and substituting the mother for a different woman. This "heterosexual" resolution, he believed, is an essential component to "normal" development. In boys, it plays out through "castration anxiety," or the fear of emasculation as punishment for their sexual fantasies. In girls, it plays out through "penis envy," or the process by which girls come to accept their own emasculation. In both cases, heterosexuality arises after successful identification with the same-sex parent.[10]

Sexual "inversion," Freud posited, arises through aberrations in psychosexual development. In the case of homosexuality, something interrupts the "heterosexual resolution" of the Oedipal stage, whether it be failure to form parental attachments properly, a traumatic sexual experience, or previous trauma in the child's life. This arresting of psychosexual development, Freud believed, can lead to pedophilia and homosexuality. Homosexual "narcissism," he said, characterizes the outcome because in failing to develop sexual attachment to the opposite-sex parent, homosexuals fixate on themselves in auto-erotic self-love.[11]

The Christian Embrace of Freud

Freud's influence in the field of psychology attained near-mythic status in the early decades of the twentieth century. Even though the concept of "homosexual" orientation was relatively new, his theories about homosexuality soon became the definitive way to talk about sexual attraction to the same sex. Words like *homosexual* and *heterosexual* entered lay vocabulary, and by 1946, the term *homosexual* made its debut in translations of Scripture.[12]

The introduction of the word *homosexual* to the Bible was earth shattering. For the first time in Christian history, the Bible now said that an entire group of people known as "homosexuals" not only existed but were also condemned. No translation prior to 1946 had ever used this word. The idea of defining a group of people by "sexual orientation" had never existed. Freud's popularization of concepts like heterosexuality, homosexuality, and bisexuality effectively cemented the concept in the public imagination. In the span of a few decades, acceptance of sexual "identity" had become so universal that Christians raised virtually no objections to this way of thinking about human identity.

The result was that in 1946 the Revised Standard Version published the following translation of 1 Corinthians 6:9–10: "Do you not know that the unrighteous will not inherit the kingdom of God? Do not be deceived; neither the immoral, nor idolators, nor adulterers, *nor homosexuals*, nor thieves, nor the greedy, nor drunkards, nor revilers, nor robbers will inherit the kingdom of God."

The above passage represents the first time the word *homosexual* was used to translate the first-century Greek words *malakoi* and *arsenokoitai* (which we'll talk about more in chapter 7), collapsing them into a single category invented by nineteenth-century sexology. The result? Scripture became "clear" on a relatively new concept overnight. Although the RSV translation team subsequently corrected their anachronism in 1972, the words *homosexual* and *homosexuality* are still found in dozens of translations of the Bible today, including the ESV, NASB, NKJV, and NLT, among others.[13]

Now, you might be thinking, *What's the big deal? Christians have always believed that same-sex intercourse is a sin. If the Bible condemns same-sex intercourse, then it condemns homosexuality. It makes sense to use this word!* But that's the thing. It doesn't. *Even if* the Bible explicitly condemns same-sex intercourse, words like *homosexual* and *homosexuality* don't belong in God's Word. The phrase *same-sex intercourse* refers to a behavior. The word *homosexual* refers to an *identity*. When we talk about homosexuality, we are no longer talking about sin but about *people*. More specifically, we're talking about a *socially constructed* category used to stigmatize and pathologize human beings.

Today, many Christians commonly perceive themselves to be stalwart defenders of biblical truth against the Freudian thinking of worldly psychology. Pastors mock psychoanalysis from the pulpit, and Christian authors bemoan the existence of sexual identity. LGBTQ people are even blamed for the existence of these categories and demonized for using them.

But Christians aided and abetted the adoption of Freudian psychology into modern culture from the very beginning, going so far as to insert the concept of homosexuality into the pages of Scripture. It was not an invention of the gay agenda, nor was it a sneaky way to normalize same-sex marriage. In fact, it first arose as a way to classify people as perverts, using sexual desire as a metric. The result was a newly constructed category for human identity defined by sexual attraction. "Heterosexuality" became the new normal, and "homosexuality" joined the Christian lexicon of sins overnight.

Reclaiming Identity from the Clutches of Stigma

Following the popularization of Freudian psychoanalysis, it didn't take long for millions of people to be clinically pathologized as psychosexually "disordered." Freud was skeptical that homosexuality could ever be remedied, but medical practitioners found within his writings a pathway to finding a "cure." In the United States, doctors forcibly subjected gays to electroshock therapy, hormone replacement, castration, and lobotomies, among other horrific practices.[14] In Nazi Germany, by the time of World War II, tens of thousands of gay men underwent forced experimentation, and over one hundred thousand were arrested, with many sent to concentration camps.[15]

Battered and stigmatized, the new class of "homosexuals" retreated into underground communities where they could escape society's hatred. It was here, in these communities, that gay men used the word *gay* for the first time and lesbian women embraced the word *lesbian*. Both terms broke away from the stigma of homosexual pathology, *gay* having a positive connotation and *lesbian* having existed long before the development of psychopathology.[16]

These two words took center stage in gay men and women's fight for equality. They weren't "homosexuals." They were gay, and they were lesbian. By the 1960s, the gay and lesbian community was asserting its identity as a *people* group deserving of respect and dignity like anybody else. They were *human beings*, not perverts and not defined by sexual degeneracy.

49

Franklin Kameny, a significant gay rights leader, described in a 1982 interview the importance of what took place. "Homosexual," he said, "was coined in the middle 1800s, and it has a very, very clinical sound. It serves its purpose. Clinicians like it, and clinicians held sway until we took back our own world in the 1960s."[17] The words *gay* and *lesbian* carried symbolic weight, a "taking back" of what had been stolen—the truth of gay people's existence as full human beings, uniquely created and no more defined by "sex and deviance" than anybody else.

Immediately, however, a public outcry erupted over the labels. "Gay activists," many said, were normalizing sexual perversion. Virtually every major Christian outlet—alongside secular outlets—insisted on using the word *homosexual* and reserved the word *gay* for derogatory comments. Others used it to evoke a bogeyman, such as wild-eyed "gay pedophiles" coming for your children. Christian editors like Joseph Farah banned the word *gay*, "the chosen term of the homosexual activists."[18] "The word 'gay,'" others protested, "has no sexual connotations."[19]

It would seem counterintuitive for Christians to embrace a word that prioritizes sex as the focal point of identity (homo*sex*ual) over a word that intentionally decenters the importance of sex (*gay*). But embracing terminology that emphasized the very thing that Christians believed to be sinful (homo*sex*uality) served a dualistic function: it maintained the social-pariah status that haunted the gay community while simultaneously justifying that status. They were perverts after all, maybe even pedophiles. Christians gravitated toward language that centered the offending trait—sex—because it maintained the pathological categories popularized by Freudian psychology but with a Christian twist.

Homosexual thus came to be the chosen language of the Christian ex-gay movement in contradistinction to the word *gay*. By focusing on gay people as homosexual sinners, Christians fell back on the Freudian depiction of gay people as psychosexually "disordered." Over time, the word *homosexual* evolved into *same-sex attracted*, and for years, the two words were used interchangeably until *same-sex attracted* became the nom du jour. Take a closer look at the two terms, and you might notice what they both have in common: the word *sex*.

The Ex-Gay Movement

Many Christians believe that ex-gay ministries represent a rejection of Freudian psychology. But in fact, the ex-gay movement relied on Freud from the start. Ex-gay darling Joseph Nicolosi, considered the founder of conversion therapy, critiqued Freud's theory of the Oedipus Complex for not accounting for the role of self-identity, but Nicolosi nevertheless concluded that Freud's basic principles were sound, including his theories of arrested development, homosexual narcissism, and parental attachment.[20] Nicolosi enjoyed speaking engagements with virtually every major Christian ex-gay ministry in his day, and his books were considered required reading for anyone seeking to overcome their "unwanted same-sex attraction," as those in ex-gay ministries often put it.

To get an idea of what ex-gay teaching looks like in everyday Christian theology, consider the following, published by Probe Ministries in 2003:

> If God had intended homosexuality to be a viable sexual alternative for some people, He would not have condemned it as an abomination. . . . Homosexuality is a manifestation of the sin nature that all people share. At the fall of man (Gen 3), God's perfect creation was spoiled, and the taint of sin affected us physically, emotionally, intellectually, spiritually—and sexually. Homosexuality is a perversion of heterosexuality, which is God's plan for His creation. . . . These people may experience "preconditions" that dispose them toward homosexuality, such

as a sensitive and gentle temperament in boys, which is not recognized as acceptably masculine in our culture. . . . Family relationships are usually very important in the development of homosexuality; the vast majority of those who struggle with same-sex attraction experienced a hurtful relationship with the same-sex parent in childhood.[21]

Here, we see how traditional beliefs about sex and marriage transform into "heterosexuality" as "God's plan for his creation." "Perversion of heterosexuality" comes to mean the same thing as "manifestation of the sin nature," which comes to mean the same as "same-sex attraction." Even the words "taint of sin" are reminiscent of Krafft-Ebing's "neuropathic taint."[22] The result is a baffling chimera of pseudoscience attached to Scripture, whereby Christians talk about abominations condemned by God as having preconditions like hurtful parental relationships.

Being a sinner in conversations about homosexuality thereby comes to mean the same thing as being a pervert in modern sexology. Christians use the language of sin and brokenness, but the talking points might as well come out of a Freudian textbook. LGBTQ people are thus subjected to forced orientation change through "a close-knit relationship with God, intensive therapy, and strong determination."[23] Extreme abuses, including electroshock therapy and sexual assault, are common.[24]

Exodus International was the flagship program for the ex-gay movement. Founded in the mid-1970s, it grew to a budget of more than one million dollars with over four hundred ministries across seventeen countries.[25] But problems riddled the organization. Cofounder Michael Bussee abandoned Exodus in 1979 to be with his lover, another Exodus leader, and admitted decades later, "I never saw one of our members or other Exodus leaders . . . become heterosexual, so deep down I knew that it wasn't true."[26] In 2000, Exodus chairman John

Paulk divorced his wife and announced, "I do not believe that reparative therapy changes sexual orientation; in fact, it does great harm to many people."[27] In 2013, president Alan Chambers issued a formal apology in which he admitted that he had "ongoing same-sex attractions" and said, "For quite some time, we've been imprisoned in a worldview that's neither honoring toward our fellow human beings, nor biblical."[28] The organization folded that year in disgrace.

About 12 percent of LGBTQ youth attempted suicide in 2019.[29] A figure that is already disproportionately high. But for LGBTQ youth who underwent conversion therapy, the number jumped to almost 30 percent.[30] A 2018 study found that children's risk of suicidal thoughts goes up by as much as 500 percent when they experience conversion therapy.[31]

Despite these troubling statistics, Christian ministries nevertheless continue to lobby for the right to use conversion therapy in biblical counseling,[32] and countless churches rely heavily upon the principles of conversion therapy and ex-gay theology in their discipleship of LGBTQ people.

You might remember Victor from earlier. Victor didn't need to get shipped off to conversion-therapy camp. Instead, ex-gay thinking colored every last inch of the wisdom he received from biblical counselors. Nobody could think of anything but getting rid of Victor's homosexuality. Homosexuality, in turn, made Victor the "pervert" in the retelling of his own molestation. Christians couldn't see the traumatized boy who had just been molested by a man who claimed to follow Jesus. All they could see was a "man of God" who could do no wrong compared to a sexual sinner who couldn't be trusted.

Ironically, in situations like Victor's, when Christians *do* recognize that the "man of God" is a rapist (which is rare), many conclude that the rapist must have been a homosexual too. The Freudian association of homosexuality with pedophilia comes full circle. The rapist is a homosexual because he's a pedophile, and the gay kid is destined to *become* a pedophile because he was homosexually raped.

Studies confirm, however, that sexual orientation has no connection to whether a person molests children.[33] LGBTQ people are *themselves* at greater risk of childhood abuse and molestation. The reason is not that sexual abuse turns people gay but, rather, that predators take advantage of LGBTQ people's vulnerability and isolation due to social stigma.[34] In Victor's case, his prior experience of attraction to people of the same sex put him in a position of vulnerability to anyone who might offer him "help" in becoming a man. Contrary to Freudian belief, Victor's traumatic experience didn't make him gay. Everybody already knew that he was gay. Instead, his gayness placed him in a position of isolation within his Christian community. It was this marginalization that created the context for abuse.

4. Freud's Lasting Influence

CAMILLA

No one was more shocked than Camilla when she dedicated her life to Christ. She had been an atheist/agnostic known for her strong dislike of anything related to church. As a Black, asexual lesbian, she viewed Christians as largely hypocritical and oppressive to marginalized people, especially when it came to queerness and race.

Then one Sunday, a few months after graduating from college, she found herself sitting in the pews of a church after losing a bet the night before. To her shock, the Holy Spirit introduced her to Jesus. By the end of the month, she had committed her life to Jesus Christ.

She joined a conservative evangelical, Reformed congregation, immersed herself in studying theology, and enrolled as an intern at her church. However, the more involved she got, the more entangled she became in a maze of rules and regulations.

"It was complementarian," she said. "So men disciple men, and women disciple women. I can only be with women. But same-sex attraction is a sin, so I can't be with women." Over time, her relationship to herself as a lesbian became increasingly shrouded by sin.

"It was clear that in order to be a Christian in the eyes of my church, I could only be asexual and celibate or I had to become straight. I didn't have any other options."

She was asexual, but she was also gay, and others in the church didn't seem to understand how this could be possible. Camilla soon found herself trying to eliminate any and all expressions of gayness in her life in a quest to become *only* asexual. Eventually, a leader that she respected told her that she couldn't be in the same bedroom with her best friend, who was also a lesbian.

"Just being in the same bedroom was a source of temptation," Camilla recalled the pastor saying. "It completely went to war against what I knew about myself and everyone else. I am so capable of being in a bedroom with someone and not jumping into their pants, and I personally don't know anybody who even has that problem. It's just bizarre."

Still, Christians told her that renouncing her same-sex attraction was essential to be holy. So she did her best to comply even as her life became increasingly defined by fear of sin.

"When I became a Christian, I knew right away that I didn't have to fear anymore, but Christians retaught me that fear," she said. "Sometimes it makes me physically nauseous. I wish that queerness had never once been talked about in relation to sin. As long as queerness and sin are put together, queer people will always hate themselves for being queer."

■ ■ ■

To borrow the favorite saying of my old apologetics professor, "All is yellow to the jaundiced eye." Indeed, the church's entanglement with psychopathology carries lasting consequences for how Christians see the world. Regardless of what many profess about identity in Christ and finding personhood through Jesus alone, when Christians meet a person attracted to the same sex, many don't see a *person*. Instead, they see a *homosexual*. A sinner. And not just any kind of sinner. A *sexual* sinner. A pervert.

Contemporary Christian writing on the subject exacerbates the problem. Rosaria Butterfield correctly criticizes the origins of sexual identity and rightly calls on Christians to reject a worldview that defines people by sexual desire.[1] However, she fails to inform her readers about the church's entanglement with sexual identity categories. Nor does she discuss the role that Christians have played in maintaining those categories. Absent is any acknowledgment of the addition of the word *homosexuality* into biblical translations following the development of psychoanalysis. Nor does she discuss how the preferred Christian language of *same-sex attraction* grew out of that legacy.

Worse, Butterfield teaches that language like *gay* and *lesbian* is the problem, claiming it to be a manifestation of people defining themselves by sexual desire, even though LGBTQ language emerged in the context of *rebellion* against sexual pathology. Confusedly, Butterfield admits her own involvement in this history. Describing her own coming-out moment, she says, "But never did I use the concept of sexual orientation to describe my sexual identity. I was a nineteenth-century scholar and I held some scholarly suspicions about this category. Also, 'sexual orientation' was not part of my lesbian, poststructural, queer culture."[2]

In other words, Butterfield acknowledges that "queer culture" is critical of sexual orientation. In fact, queer theory provides some of the strongest critiques of Freudian psychology.[3] Nevertheless, Butterfield guides her readers to believe that LGBTQ language reflects the vices of a community that supposedly defines their identity by sex.

Other writers share similar contradictions. Denny Burk, professor of biblical studies at Boyce College and president of the Council for Biblical Manhood and Womanhood, admits that "queer theorists are rejecting [sexual orientation] as a fixed identity marker" and are "destabilizing the concept of sexual orientation as identity."[4] Nevertheless, even though he admits that queer theory deconstructs sexual identity, Burk *still* tries to convince readers that gay and lesbian people make their "sexual attractions the touchstone of [their] being."[5] He ends up accusing queer people of the very thing he admits they reject.

It amounts to spilling your coffee all over your friend in order to accuse them of being messy. By reducing the gay identity to nothing more than "the sum total of fallen sexual desire,"[6] Burk defines gay people by disordered sexual desire in order to tell gay people to stop defining themselves by disordered sexual desire. The result is a reductionistic portrayal of the gay identity wherein Burk insists that to identify as *gay* is to identify with *sin*. However, it's not actually gay people who define themselves in this way. It's Burk who defines gay people by *sex* and thereby concludes that gay people are defined by *sin*.

As illogical as it is, Burk's approach is shockingly common. Consider Camilla's experience. It didn't matter to her church that she was asexual. She was a *lesbian* and that meant she was embracing a *sinful sexual identity*. Her church interpreted *all* of Camilla's behavior through the lens of sexual perversion even though Camilla never experienced sexual attraction. She wound up contorting her life into ridiculous restrictions, like never entering the same bedroom as a lesbian, all for the sake of rooting out her "same-sex attraction." Never mind that she didn't experience sexual desire. If she was gay, something *had* to be sinful. Without a framework to conceive of the gay experience outside of sexual perversion, her sexuality carried the potential for sin and only sin.

The Fight to Be Seen

Any LGBTQ person knows that a key struggle is getting outsiders to see them as full human beings, not defined by gender or sexual "deviance." Out of the hundreds of LGBTQ people that I know, inside and outside the church, I've yet to meet a single person who says their gender or sexuality "defines" them in the way that Butterfield, Burk, and others claim. In fact, many discuss the ways in which their identity is so much more than gender and sexuality and the challenge of getting people to see them as such.

This confuses many Christians: *If LGBTQ people don't want to be defined by their sex or gender identity, then why do they insist on identifying as LGBTQ?* In order to understand the answer to this question, it's important to understand the *function* of LGBTQ language. Gay people don't call themselves gay and lesbian because they define themselves by sex. Rather, such language is a *response* to the sexual stigma of society. As long as LGBTQ people experience dehumanization on the basis of sex and gender, they will need a vocabulary to name that experience and ultimately reclaim their humanity.

Queer language therefore challenges how the world would otherwise define the queer experience. Sometimes this means providing alternative words to stigmatizing labels. Gay people are not "homosexual" or "same-sex attracted," for example. They are gay, and they are lesbian. At other points, it means reclaiming words that were slurs. In using the word *queer*, for example, LGBTQ people turn the tables on bigotry, robbing it of power. Queer theorists stubbornly refuse to define what *queer* even means, insisting that its definition is in *not* having a definition, in pushing back against reductionistic labels in the first place.[7] Contained within queer language is always a correction to stigma and a cry for justice.

When LGBTQ people say to loved ones, "This is who I am," a phrase that Butterfield criticizes,[8] they are pleading to be seen. Far from defining themselves by gender and sexuality, they are asking for their *full humanity* to be acknowledged.

What then does it mean to be gay? Gay people talk freely about their "gay wardrobe" and their "gay haircut" as well as their "gay music" and "gay handwriting." I've had friends post captions on social media like "My Gay Agenda" underneath a shot of a vegan grocery list. Such comments, though tongue-in-cheek, subvert popular stereotypes of who gay people are and what they want out of their lives by reminding the world that to be gay is to be human. To inhabit the world differently than the vast majority of people but no less made in the image of God and no more reducible to any single aspect of life.

Most importantly, gay people use the word *gay* to describe how they find themselves relationally situated in the world. It might describe sexual attraction but not necessarily (asexual people like Camilla can be just as gay as RuPaul). Indeed, queer culture challenges the notion that sexuality is only or even primarily about sex. Instead, it describes a broader *relational* experience, one that is *not* just sexual but includes emotional, romantic, aesthetic, physical, and intellectual components, among others. These experiences impact everything about how any person relates to the world, but they don't define who we are or what we do with our lives. They add color to our existence, but they don't govern it.

In this sense, the gay experience is not so much a sexual experience as it is a *relational* experience. Gay people like Camilla can be asexual, and asexual people can be gay because the gay experience evades reductionism. It demands to be *more*. In his autobiographical play that chronicles gay activism during the AIDS epidemic, Larry Kramer says the following: "The only way we'll have real pride is when we demand recognition of a culture that isn't just sexual. It's all there—all through history we've been there; but we have to claim it, and identify who was in it, and articulate what's in our minds and hearts and all our creative contributions to this earth. . . . Being defined by our cocks is literally killing us."[9]

Kramer's words get to the heart of gay activism: a rejection of being "defined by our cocks," an assertion of human dignity. Gay scholar David Halperin puts it this way: "Gay identity cannot express gay desire or gay subjectivity because gay desire is not limited to desire for men. . . . Gay male desire actually comprises a kaleidoscopic range of queer longings—of wishes and sensations and pleasures and emotions—that exceed the bounds of any singular identity and extend beyond the specifics of gay male existence."[10] Although Halperin is speaking of the gay male experience, his words hold true for the broad range of experiences contained within LGBTQ people's lived reality.

Indeed, to be queer is to participate in a shared culture uniquely shaped by existing at the margins of society. This leads to a phenomenological experience that only queer people inhabit and that contributes to the diversity of the world. By existing at the margins, queer people reimagine things in ways that straight and cisgender people can't, and they think outside the boxes of majority culture. These experiences may be in the minority, but they are *human* experiences nevertheless.

To be queer is to be human.

Reducing Queer People to Sinners

The greatest irony of all is that while many Christians insist on a definition of the gay experience that reduces to sex, many simultaneously point the finger at sexual minorities and accuse *them* of defining their identity by sex. Whereas the word *gay* has a broad meaning that gay Christians understand to include the possibility of unique sins and temptations as well as unique blessings and goodness (as does the word *straight*), many Christians reimagine the term to only include the possibility of sin and temptation. By reducing the gay identity to sin, Christians redefine queer language to reinforce the very categories that such language was meant to subvert, thereby blaming gay believers for the stigma that Christians themselves reproduce.

All people sin. Straight people no less than gay. However, in the context of homosexuality, the word *sinner* transforms into something very different from what Christians mean when they say, "I'm just a sinner saved by grace." Consider just a few of the sound bites that many Christians say to gay believers: "There's no such thing as a gay Christian!" "Would you call yourself a murdering Christian? No? Why call yourself a gay Christian then?" "'Gay Christian' is an oxymoron!"

These casually dismissive statements make clear that such Christians see gay people as "sinners" very differently than how they see themselves as "sinners." One is a sinner in that they happen to sin, and that's why Jesus died and rose again. The other is a sinner in that they couldn't possibly follow Jesus. One is biblical. The other is pathological.

The same can be said for how Christians talk about "the fall." Every aspect of the human condition is fallen. But in the context of queerness, being "fallen" takes on a different meaning than what Christians suggest when they say that straight and cisgender people are fallen. One is fallen in that cisgender heterosexuality carries the potential to sin as well as the potential to live in faithfulness to God. The other is fallen in that queerness carries the potential to sin and only sin. One is fallen in the sense that God saves it. The other is fallen in the sense that God hates it.

In this approach, there's absolutely nothing redeemable about the queer experience. In fact, it is the "opposite of holiness."[11] God has no purpose for it. As a result, in the minds of many Christians, as long as LGBTQ people are queer, they cannot be holy. They exist in a perpetual state of sin for which they must perpetually repent until they cease to be queer altogether. It's therefore no surprise that many LGBTQ Christians die by suicide or face suicidal thoughts. Unable to rid their existence of queerness, they are tempted to rid *themselves* of their *existence*.

BURDEN 2 SUMMARY

We thus conclude the second burden that LGBTQ people bear in the church. No matter what queer people do, how they live, how they talk, or how they define their own existence, when many Christians meet an LGBTQ person they see a pathological sinner. A pervert. All people sin, but LGBTQ people are sinners without grace.

BURDEN 3
FOLK DEVILS

5. Political Christianity

LILY

Lily grew up going to church every Sunday with her Chinese-American family. She never got too involved in things outside Sunday morning service until age thirteen, when she started attending a new Sunday school. She got to know some of the kids, and eventually a friend's father invited her over to their family's house.

When she arrived, it was just her and her friend's dad.

"He told me he wanted to have sex with me," Lily recalled. "I told him, 'No.'" After seeing that Lily would not have sex with him, he decided to let her go, but Lily was traumatized. She went home and told her father, but he didn't know how to respond. The man had recently befriended him at church. He didn't want to cause trouble.

In the end, nothing happened to the man until Lily turned eighteen and started dating the church's youth pastor. Now her boyfriend, the youth pastor kicked Lily's former predator out of the church, but he himself slept with congregants under his care, including Lily.

"I really didn't understand that there was a power differential," Lily said. "I still don't fully understand the dynamics that were at play." Another woman in the congregation, who had previously slept with the youth pastor, reported him to a different pastor. They all met together, but the additional pastor offered little guidance.

"He could have said something," Lily said. "He could have told the youth pastor to consider his position over me and consider his sleeping around in the congregation and how that was affecting the congregation."

Lily eventually broke up with him, graduated from college, and started attending a new church. One of the ministry leaders invited Lily to join a small group. After sessions, he started asking Lily to meet for one-on-ones, which turned into dinners and eventually movies at his place.

He was twice her age, and she was still coming to terms with her bisexuality. Uncomfortable with the intimate direction their sessions had taken, Lily asked to bring her sister along.

"He completely flipped out," Lily recalled. "And he told me that I would no longer be allowed to attend the small group." Lily eventually left the church.

DEAN

Dean had years of experience working with children in full-time ministry, starting off as a family ministries intern, directing the children's choir and theater workshop, and eventually accepting a position as the elementary children's ministry director at a large Independent Christian Church. Everything was going great until he shared his testimony with the pastors and came out as gay.

He was heterosexually married and faithful to his wife, so he didn't think it would be a big deal. But shortly thereafter they reassigned him from his role as children's ministry director to a newly created position over LGBTQ outreach, and nobody would let him do anything around children. When he asked about it, they said, "We just don't think it's wise." Nobody accused him of pedophilia. "We just don't want people *thinking* you're a pedophile," they said.

Accusations of pedophilia, or what his church described as protection from accusations of pedophilia, followed him everywhere he went until he found himself getting anxious around children. "Being told over and over again, almost monthly, 'Be careful, you don't want people to suspect you're a pedophile,' conditioned me," Dean explained. "I was always thinking of how someone could accuse me of something."

Over time, Dean found his life subjected to greater and greater scrutiny. He volunteered to go on a trip to a conference, and the pastor asked if the only reason he wanted to go was because he had secret feelings for the staff member in charge. On a different occasion, he posted a photo of himself and a friend on social media, and the pastor demanded to know what he meant by sharing the picture.

"It got to the point where I couldn't talk about my personal life," Dean said. "Anything I said could and would be used against me."

Meanwhile, straight men at Dean's church interacted with children alone without any concerns or background checks. It made Dean wonder. How many real sexual predators might be slipping through the cracks of his church because they didn't fit the "profile"? People at his church were so busy worrying about Dean. How many people were exhibiting real signs of sexual predation that no one bothered to notice?

■ ■ ■

When the #MeToo movement took off in 2017, it didn't take long for evangelical Christianity to face its own reckoning. Stories of sexual abuse in Christian communities flooded social media, categorized under #ChurchToo. The crisis extended as far as—if not further than—the Catholic sex abuse scandal in the early 2000s, and investigations only deepened the crisis.

Registered sex offenders had been allowed to lead entire ministries under the guise of having "repented," only to molest children for years. Rape victims had been told to forgive their assailants instead of calling the police. In one case, in the living room of a family's home and surrounded by people, a young man masturbated with a little girl in his lap.[1]

An investigative report from the *Houston Chronicle* found that hundreds of pastors within the Southern Baptist Convention (SBC) had engaged in sexual misconduct with over seven hundred victims over a period of twenty years.[2] At least 218 SBC leaders had pled guilty or been convicted of sex crimes, with many more credibly accused but never removed from leadership. Others had been allowed to keep their ordination and relocate to new churches.[3]

Previously ignored studies resurfaced with alarming statistics, showing that 70 percent of Southern Baptist ministers "knew of other ministers who had sexual contact with a parishioner."[4] One survey found that between 10 and 38 percent of respondents admitted to engaging in some type of sexual misconduct with church members.[5] Another study showed that 23 percent of evangelical ministers "admitted to engaging in sexually inappropriate conduct" with congregants.[6] Another study estimated that seven women *per congregation* will experience clergy sexual misconduct in any given year in the US.[7]

The statistics are shocking, but many seemed incapable of admitting that a problem might exist.[8] In the time leading up to the *Houston Chronicle* report, the most common response amounted to essentially, "Forgive and forget."

Among the most poignant examples, in late 2017, Andy Savage found himself accused of sexually assaulting a minor during his previous tenure as a youth pastor at a church in Texas. Savage confessed to his church and said that he was "deeply sorry." In response, the congregation erupted into applause.[9] As of the writing of this book, he remains ordained in the Southern Baptist Convention and is planning to start a new church.[10] Baffling as it is that a pastor guilty of sexual assault might receive a round of applause for simply saying, "I'm sorry," Savage's praise looks even more bewildering in light of events just a few months later.

In late 2017 and early 2018, a group of gay Christians were organizing a new conference called Revoice to "support, encourage, and empower gay, lesbian, same-sex-attracted, and other LGBT Christians so they can flourish while observing the historic, Christian doctrine of marriage and sexuality."[11] The goal was to help LGBTQ people pursue chastity as traditionally defined. You'd think conservative evangelicals would celebrate it. Instead, Revoice organizers received immediate and unrelenting backlash from virtually every corner of the church. Robert Gagnon, professor of New Testament theology at Houston Baptist University, wrote in response to the conference that LGBTQ identities "cannot be sanctified."[12] Denny Burk rejected the idea that queer culture was "redeemable."[13] Albert Mohler stated that LGBTQ culture is "defined *in its essence* by the rejection of God's design and command" and that "Revoice is not the voice of faithful Christianity."[14]

Where silence reigned in the context of the sex abuse crisis unfolding in real time in evangelical circles, Christian leaders emerged out of the woodwork to condemn a conference for gay people committed to chastity.

How did we get there?

The Gay Folk Devil

"Folk devils" were first described in 1972 by sociologist Stanley Cohen. In his now classic book *Folk Devils and Moral Panic*, Cohen studied the UK media frenzy surrounding the mods and rockers in 1960s Great Britain, showing how public rhetoric served to villainize and blame the two subcultures for perceptions of moral decline in British youth. The mods and rockers, he said, were a folk devil.[15]

Folk devils stoke the fires of moral panic.[16] They symbolize the fears of the masses and become a channel for public anxiety, regardless of their actual responsibility for the problems at hand. Sensationalized rhetoric distorts public perception of the maligned "folk devil" group, collapsing all members into a single "type" that fuels a moral crusade, however fabricated, for political and social change.

Folk devils abound throughout history. Jewish people were a "folk devil" in Nazi Germany. So too were deviant women

71

during the Salem witch trials. In both cases, it mattered little whether Jewish people or deviant women were actual threats to society. What mattered was the public perception of a threat and the need for someone to blame. In the abstract world of perceived moral decline and social instability, folk devils give people a *tangible* enemy to defeat.

In the context of the 1970s and '80s, facing the consequences of rapid cultural change and diminishing political influence, conservative leaders began to organize Christians against a growing litany of moralized "others." Political rhetoric cast the nation in a battle over Christian family values. Man-hating feminists, "crazy" abortionists, and "homosexual pedophiles" came to increasingly define the moral enemy. The "gay agenda" loomed over it all, the culmination of a godless culture that would corrupt children and destroy America.[17]

"So-called gay folks would just as soon kill you as look at you," Jerry Falwell said at a 1977 rally in Miami, igniting the "Save Our Children" campaign.[18] Pitting gay civil rights against the safety of families, the campaign argued that local ordinances protecting gay people from employment discrimination foreshadowed the corrupting of America's youth. In a 1977 letter to Californians, the Reverend Louis P. Sheldon, a Presbyterian minister, called on the public to vote against a piece of legislation that would protect gay teachers from losing their employment. "Already mobs of militant homosexuals have taken to the streets," he wrote. "The children of California need our help now. We must not let them down."[19]

In a postscript to the same letter, he attached a newspaper clipping to "give you an idea of what we are up against." "Take a good look at the man in the *Times* photo who is wearing an earring and fingernail polish," he said. "Ask yourself this question, 'Is this the kind of man I want teaching my children?'"[20]

Such rhetoric galvanized voters like few issues could, bringing them out in the hundreds of thousands to vote against gay rights legislation and buoying the formation of Falwell's Moral Majority two years later. "The homosexuals are on the march in this country," wrote Falwell in 1981. "Please remember, homosexuals do not reproduce! They recruit! And, many of them are after my children and your children."[21]

In painting gay people as a monolithic, recruiting enemy, Falwell proved to be the strongest recruiter himself. By the start of the 1980s, the gay folk devil had become such a powerful symbol in the hands of political leaders that they could easily harness it to arouse fear, anger, and hostility among religious-minded voters.

AIDS, Hellfire, and Tragedy

Ruth Koker Burks saw the door with a red bag taped over it for the first time in 1984. She had been spending hours in and out of University Hospital in Little Rock, Arkansas, with a friend who had cancer.[22] Trays of uneaten food lay forgotten beside the red door, and nurses drew straws to see who would go inside.[23] No one mentioned what was hiding behind the door. But Ruth knew.[24]

Twenty-five years old and the mother of a girl still in diapers, Ruth had started to hear rumors of a "gay cancer" plaguing the nation. Sitting in the hallway, where she was waiting to visit her friend, she overheard the nurses arguing over who should go through the red door. She decided to ask about the room.

"He's got the gay disease," the nurses said. "We don't even know what it is. Don't you go in there."[25]

Pushing past a sign that said "Do Not Enter," Ruth opened the door to discover a young man shriveled away to barely more than a skeleton. "He was so frail and so pale and so near death. And he weighed less than 100 pounds," Ruth said. "And you couldn't really tell him from the sheets on the bed."[26] His name was Jimmy. Ruth took up his hand in her own and gave his arm a gentle rub before asking, "Is there anything I can do for you?"[27] He told her he wanted his mama.

Ruth went back out to the hallway and found the group of nurses.

"Did you go into that room?" one said incredulously. "Have you lost your mind? Do you know what's happening?"[28] So little was known about the disease that even healthcare workers feared catching it by simply entering the same room as an infected patient.

One of the nurses eventually gave Ruth the number for Jimmy's mom. But within a few seconds of Ruth calling, the woman on the other end hung up.[29]

Ruth wasn't having it. "I called her back," she said. "I said, 'If you hang up on me again, I will put your son's obituary in your hometown newspaper and I will list his cause of death.' Then I had her attention."[30] The *Arkansas Times* describes what happened next: "Her son was a sinner, the woman told [Ruth]. She didn't know what was wrong with him and didn't care. She wouldn't come, as he was already dead to her as far as she was concerned. She said she wouldn't even claim his body when he died. It was a hymn [Ruth] would hear again and again over the next decade: sure judgment and yawning hellfire, abandonment on a platter of scripture."[31]

Ruth walked back into the room to tell Jimmy his mother wasn't coming. But before she could find the words, he raised his hand weakly and called out to her, "Oh momma, I knew you'd come." She took up his hand in her own and said, "I'm here, honey. I'm here," and she sat with him the rest of the night.[32] Thirteen hours later, he died.

No one came to mourn Jimmy, and no cemetery would accept his ashes. She called around to every church in the area, asking for a minister to pray over his grave. Everyone refused. She went out to her family's private cemetery and dug the grave on her own. "I couldn't even get anyone to come dig a hole for me," she said.[33]

Over the next three decades, Ruth cared for over a thousand patients dying of AIDS, burying many of them on her own property, using cookie jars for their ashes.[34] No priest or pastor would pray for them, though she begged repeatedly. "I tried every time," she recalled. "They hung up on me. They cussed me out. They prayed like I was a demon on the phone and they had to get me off—prayed while they were on the phone. Just crazy. Just ridiculous."[35] Out of a thousand gay men, three had family members step forward.[36] "You were the only person that we could call," remembered one survivor. "There wasn't anyone. It was just you."[37] The KKK burned crosses in her yard on three separate occasions.[38]

The emotional toll was devastating. Perhaps because she was a mother herself, Ruth recalled in painful detail the rejection that so many of the men experienced from their families. One man named Billy broke down in the middle of a mall and wept in Ruth's arms.[39] For most, she was the closest thing to a mother they had. As reported in the *Arkansas Times*, "[One man] had so much fluid in his lungs that he couldn't breathe. He couldn't talk, and he would gag when he was trying to talk. His mother, we had called and called and called. . . . He wanted to talk to his mother and wanted me to try again. I got the answering machine, and I just handed the phone to him. He cried and gagged. It was excruciating listening to him ask his mother if she'd come to the hospital. She never came."[40]

Another woman called up Burks and demanded to know how much longer she would have to wait for her son to just die already. "I just want to know, when is he going to die?" the woman said. "We have to get on with our lives. . . . He's ruined our lives."[41]

When AIDS patients died, hospital workers walked into the room wearing hazmat suits to clear it out. It was common for dying men to be left to fend for themselves, even in hospitals. Nurses refused to enter rooms, leaving food outside for the dying men to fetch on their own.[42] "I was in an abandoned part of the ward," one survivor recalled. "I was by myself with signs on my door saying, 'Hazard.'"[43]

Healthy men, often young, were falling ill and dying with little explanation. Purple lesions would appear on their skin, and four months later, they'd be dead. Or they'd wake up in the middle of the night vomiting blood and die a few days later. Or they'd slowly waste away over the years to a shadow of their former self until they breathed their last, alone in an empty hospital room.

"I was seeing all my friends dying around me," a survivor recalled. "Friend after friend after friend was dying."[44] One gay man estimated that he had an inner circle of about forty friends when he first tested positive for HIV in 1985. Twenty were dead within six years. Only three survived long-term. "I was in San Francisco hoping no one would die there," said one man. "And then they all died. Then I moved to Provincetown, and they all died."[45] Another survivor cried as he recalled, "All those people were supposed to be with me for the rest of my life."[46]

We now recognize HIV as an early harbinger of a much broader public health trend where novel viruses and antibiotic resistant bacteria are increasingly common. Though AIDS didn't originate in the gay community, it hit gay men the hardest in the United States. Around the globe, it impacted people from all walks of life, regardless of gender or sexual orientation. By the end of the decade, tens of thousands of people were dead from the disease in North America alone. By the end of the next decade, it was hundreds of thousands in North America and millions globally. The World Health Organization listed it as the fourth leading cause of death worldwide.[47] Today, it remains the leading global cause of death among women of reproductive age, claiming hundreds of thousands of lives every year.

Nevertheless, because US citizens so closely associated AIDS with homosexuality, much of the world dismissed it as a "gay problem," believing it to be self-inflicted. One of the first articles about AIDS, published in 1981 by the *New York Times*, ran with the headline, "Rare cancer seen in 41 homosexuals."[48] Public health experts frequently referred to it as "GRID," or "Gay-Related Immune Deficiency." It took years for experts to acknowledge that the disease was *also* infecting and killing *heterosexual* people by the millions in sub-Saharan Africa.[49] Even then, many blamed African sexual promiscuity for the spread, as though heterosexual people in the West were somehow less promiscuous.[50]

Regardless of any perceived connection to a "promiscuous lifestyle," it's difficult to fathom that in a Bible Belt city with numerous pastors, priests, ministers, and other Christian leaders, Ruth couldn't find a single one to minister to the men she cared for. How could Christians turn their backs on desperate and dying people? During a church meeting, Ruth proposed the idea of a gay support group using one of their Sunday school classrooms. In response, the pastor said, "Surely you aren't talking about bringing *those people* into this church, are you?"[51]

6. Hellfire and Judgment

JONAH

Jonah had been working as a counselor at a Christian youth camp for over three years. The directors pegged him for a position on the leadership team in charge of managing other counselors. He loved his job, and they loved him. Until he came out.

"I thought it would be fine," Jonah recalled. "I didn't think there would be any problems. I had this false sense of security that Christians love people." An article by a celibate, same-sex-attracted Christian argued that discrimination in the church was rare and that most gay people, if they abide by traditional teaching on sexual ethics, would be accepted by other Christians. Jonah was celibate, so he thought he'd be fine. Instead, he was fired.

His supervisor called him up on the phone that week and grilled him about his sexuality. When the conversation concluded, the supervisor informed Jonah that he would no longer be working for the camp. "I said, 'Wait, are you really going to fire me because I'm gay?'" Jonah recalled. The supervisor responded, "It's not about that at all."

"The conversation was all about sexuality," Jonah said, "but then once I asked if they were actually firing me because of my sexuality, it was, 'Oh no, no, no, no!' and then all of these other reasons suddenly appeared out of thin air."

Jonah approached his church for support but found that some in the congregation were discussing whether Jonah was a pedophile, if he was living in sin for identifying as "gay" instead of "same-sex attracted," and floating a proposition to explicitly bar same-sex-attracted people from volunteering in youth ministry, which the church eventually adopted.

"I was repeatedly treated more like an idea than a person," Jonah said. He had a bottle of wine and ninety-six pills spread out on the surface of his desk. "Everything was numb. I was literally just existing." He couldn't see another way out.

■ ■ ■

When news of a "gay plague" hit the press in 1981, declarations of God's judgment swiftly followed. Such condemnations reinforced the moralistic political narrative that religious leaders had created, solidifying the gay community as a symbolic stage on which traditional morality could be demonstrated. Gay people were abandoned and left to die for the sake of teaching the world a moral lesson.

A number of denominations eventually took steps in the second half of the decade to respond compassionately.[1] But such measures among more liberal denominations served as fodder for conservative groups, proof that the "homosexual agenda" was infiltrating the church.

The gay community thus became a political volleyball in the growing culture wars. The Moral Majority lobbied against government-funded research to find a cure for the new disease, arguing that AIDS was God's judgment.[2] At one point, Jerry Falwell compared the gay community to the ancient Egyptian army being drowned by God in the Red Sea.[3] Charles Stanley, then head of the Southern Baptist Convention, responded to the tragic death of movie star Rock Hudson by complaining, "It's almost as if he's becoming more heroic dying of AIDS, with all the publicity he's gotten."[4] The Reverend Billy Graham, in front of an audience of forty thousand people, asked rhetorically,

"Is AIDS a judgment of God?" before concluding that it was.[5] Years later he retracted this statement, but the damage was done. Christians in the medical community, given the lack of concrete scientific information about AIDS, filled the void by quoting Scripture in the absence of data. One Christian medical professional, writing for the *Southern Medical Journal*, supposed that it was only "logical" that AIDS be a "self-inflicted disorder" and a "due penalty of error."[6]

In a cultural climate where the religious right had coalesced into the single most powerful voting bloc in US society, such rhetoric shaped how entire government administrations responded to the AIDS crisis. In the United States, the Reagan administration treated the matter as if it were a joke.[7] White House press conferences erupted in laughter whenever the subject of AIDS was even mentioned.[8] Across the ocean, leaders in African countries never considered that they might be facing the same epidemic. When it was finally suggested, many scoffed, thinking that a "gay disease" couldn't afflict their own people.[9]

In a world where AIDS was a "gay problem" and gay people expendable, it was presumed that "homosexuals should solve their own problems."[10] After all, whatever problems they faced, they clearly deserved. During a 1984 radio broadcast of his "Old Time Gospel Hour," Falwell said that gay people were "brute beasts, part of a vile and satanic system."[11] In a 1987 memoir, Falwell bragged about humiliating his childhood gym teacher, who was gay and who "pranced about" giving orders to students. "I led the growing resistance movement to this teacher and his prissy falsetto ways," Falwell said.

> Suddenly I tackled him and began to wrestle him toward the sports equipment storage room. Two other students finally helped me subdue him, while the rest of the class looked on in shocked surprise. Inside the storage room, I pinned him to the

floor. With the aid of my classmates, I pulled off his britches and left him pantless in a bin of basketballs. After locking the gym teacher in his own storage area, I took his pants to the school's main bulletin board in the front lobby and pinned them up with a note reading "Mr. ———'s britches."

Falwell then bragged about going to the principal's office the next day, where he and the principal had such a good laugh about it that the principal "almost fell out of his chair."[12]

Such stories (which Falwell shared openly with his readers) expose the degree to which many Christians saw gay people as the butt of jokes, their lives as having little consequence, and their punishment as a just reward. Gay people thus found themselves removed from the reach of God's grace and redefined as a monstrous "other," deserving of suffering in this life and damnation in the life to come.

Lasting Effects

In 2016, a gunman entered Pulse nightclub in Orlando and killed forty-nine people and wounded fifty-three more; most of the victims were LGBTQ people of Latin-American descent. As a mixed-race Puerto Rican, I found myself shaken to the core. Had I lived in Orlando, I could have easily been among the dead. And yet in the days thereafter, a pastor got up in front of his congregation and said, "Are you sad that 50 pedophiles were killed today? Um—no—I think that's great! I think that helps society. I think Florida is a little safer tonight." Later in the sermon, he said, "If we lived in a righteous government, they should round them all up and put them up against a firing wall, and blow their brains out."[13]

Another Christian ministry suggested that the victims had knowingly waltzed into harm's way. The author pointed out that Satan is like a roaring lion seeking whom he may devour, and said, "Just ask the parents of the ones who died at the Pulse nightclub."[14]

The gay folk devil remains a compelling and powerful illusion in the imagination of Christians today, resurfacing time and time again, relying on the same worn-out narratives, reinforced by the same tropes. Coming to terms with this reality is not about casting blame. It's about taking stock of the framework for thinking about LGBTQ people that a generation of Christian leaders passed down to us. It's about honestly assessing how this framework continues to shape our thinking.

In the aftermath of the Orlando shooting, Christians whom I personally know debated whether visiting Orlando to offer condolences to the LGBTQ community might signal support for a "sinful" lifestyle. In the 2016 election, I saw friends argue that LGBTQ people represent a threat to religious liberty and must therefore be fought. A few years ago, a friend of mine told me they believed that punishing homosexuality with the death penalty would improve society. A week ago someone that I've known for over a decade sent me a long message in which they told me that, as a lesbian, I was on a satanic path that would lead me to "hang out with liberals and absorb their values" and "traverse the circles of hell."

Many assume that the apparent contradiction of the term *gay Christian* is embedded in the definition of the word *gay*. In reality, it's deeply embedded in anti-gay sentiment. Queer culture, many teach, is "in its essence" a "rejection of God's design."[15] "Redeeming" queer culture is impossible.[16] LGBTQ identities "cannot be sanctified."[17] Butterfield puts scare quotes around the word *Christian* when talking about LGBTQ believers.[18] Mohler states that there is "no such thing as a gay Christian" and that "gay Christians do not exist."[19]

At the beginning of chapter 5, I asked how a pastor guilty of sexual assault could receive a standing ovation in 2017 but a gay Christian conference dedicated to traditional morality could get nothing but condemnation. The answer lies in decades-old typecasting.

Religious-political leaders have intentionally preyed upon the moral anxieties of everyday Christians and given them queer people to blame. In so doing, Christian leaders have defined the queer community as the embodiment of immorality. Queer people find themselves to be pagans and heretics not because they *are* but because Christians have decided to see them that way.

I'm reminded of Dean's story. After a lifetime of successful work in family and children's ministry, coming out as *gay* a few years ago was the disqualifying event that subjected him to unrelenting scrutiny and suspicion, to the point that he could not even volunteer to participate in ministry events without raising eyebrows. Meanwhile, straight men at Dean's church interacted with children in potentially compromising situations without so much as a background check.

What is the likelihood that a predator was allowed to roam free in their midst while everyone worried about the gay guy? What is the cost of allowing such prejudices to determine church policies instead of training people to recognize the actual signs of predatory behavior?

We already know the answer. Hundreds upon hundreds of pastors have been implicated in sex abuse cover-ups in the past four years alone, and these are only the tip of the iceberg. Many more will never be exposed. And yet even as the #Church-Too movement was exploding in 2017, with new allegations surfacing by the day, leading evangelical voices *still* remained completely distracted by a bunch of gay people attending a conference called Revoice.

Indeed, the concept of a *gay* conference dedicated to "traditional Christian values" is impossible in the minds of many. Gay people *can't* be Christian, much less embody "traditional values." People responded so violently to the concept of a gay conference committed to chastity because the very *idea* of it offends the anti-gay political structures created by Christians in the first place.

I'm reminded of Jonah's story. Believing that most Christians merely object to progressive sexual ethics as opposed to gay people themselves, he came out as gay and celibate to his conservative Christian community. But it didn't matter that he was celibate. He still lost his job and was barred from ministry. Stories like Jonah's expose a hard truth. Underneath all the talk about "family values" and "biblical teaching," a much more hostile commitment lingers. Even *if* LGBTQ people go by the rulebook, commit to celibacy, and follow traditional teaching, it's often not enough. At the end of the day, it's not progressivism that many oppose. It's LGBTQ people themselves.

BURDEN 3 SUMMARY

We conclude the third burden that LGBTQ people bear in the church. When it comes to LGBTQ issues, many Christians are more committed to being enemies than to embodying the truth of the gospel. The cost of defining an entire group of people as the moral enemy is moral blindness.

BURDEN 4

THE BIBLE IS "CLEAR"

7. Culture and Context

EMILY

People rarely talked about homosexuality in Emily's church. Growing up in an evangelical family, Emily never considered that she could be gay herself because, well, she couldn't. She was a Christian.

But she also knew that she was different. Those differences piled up until finally as a teenager, she realized that she was gay. "It was jarring. Blindsiding," Emily recalled. "The experience of feeling a certain way and knowing that I was oriented a certain way, but also trying to reconcile that with still believing that homosexuality was wrong, but then realizing that it wasn't something that I could help—it was unbelievably confusing."

When she started working as a young adult, her coworkers tried to help. But they weren't Christians, and they couldn't understand what she needed. "They were looking at it from a completely secular viewpoint," Emily recalled, "so they didn't have any useful advice for me trying to reconcile my faith and sexuality. At the same time, nobody who shared my faith had anything helpful to say either. I knew there must be a bridge somewhere. But it was like asking for directions and people responding with completely irrelevant answers."

Still living at home, Emily tried her best to keep her parents from finding out that she was gay. But a stray text message caught her mother's eye. In a matter of days, the bottom fell out of Emily's life. "It was super sudden," she recalled. "I didn't have time to process."

Soon thereafter, Emily disappeared from the outside world—an experience shared by many LGBTQ people whose families, not wanting to kick them out of their homes, go to the other extreme and keep them locked up. Unable to go to work, Emily lost her job and was lectured daily about sin, pedophilia, and sexual perversion, isolated behind the walls of their home for weeks that turned into months.

"I couldn't see anybody," she recalled. "I started thinking of good ways to kill myself."

Worried by Emily's disappearance, her former coworkers called the police, but when the cops arrived at Emily's house, she told them everything was fine. "I was so afraid. I didn't want to hurt my family."

Technically, she could leave whenever she wanted. She was an adult after all. But she also knew that leaving apart from her parents' blessing was unacceptable. She felt trapped. Like there was no way out but death.

That startled Emily. Was she really so afraid of hurting her parents that she'd rather perish under their authority than find a better way?

Seizing on a rare moment when she was alone, she climbed through her bedroom window and ran away.

■ ■ ■

Most of the LGBTQ people I interviewed for this book (over two dozen) shared striking similarities. Most had been told that LGBTQ people go to hell. Most had learned that even experiencing same-sex attraction is inherently sinful and that using LGBTQ terminology to describe their experience is a disgrace to their Christian identity. Most told me harrowing stories of being kicked out of churches and ministries, losing friends, losing jobs, facing false accusations, and enduring hours of interrogation about the smallest details of their personal lives. They learned to see themselves as inherently perverted *just* for experiencing gender and sexuality in ways that differ from the cisgender, heterosexual majority. These patterns hold true not just for the people I interviewed but also for the hundreds of LGBTQ people that I know personally. As I mentioned already, for every story I share in this book, a thousand more exist just like it. I am not describing exceptional cases. I am describing the norm.

In particular, almost every person I interviewed in the past year began their story in the same place: *Good Christians don't ask questions about homosexuality or any other LGBTQ issue.* "The Bible is clear," the thinking goes. Questions about a Scripture passage's context, the original intent, or the merits of different interpretations are off the table. Homosexuality is a sin, end of story.

But most Christians don't treat other interpretive issues in this way. In my church growing up, I learned that context was crucial. Our pastor preached expository sermons in which he went through the books of the Bible verse by verse, sometimes spending multiple weeks on a single sentence to elucidate its meaning. Every Sunday I could expect him to walk us through a careful exegetical journey of each word in each sentence, explaining not only the historical and cultural context but also the meaning of the original word and its use in other passages, always with an eye for the author's original intent.

But for some reason, many Christians have an almost allergic reaction to context when it comes to homosexuality. Many will quote 1 Corinthians 6:9–10, which says that the "effeminate" (KJV) and "homosexuals" (NKJV) won't inherit the kingdom of heaven, and quickly call it a day. If a gay person even mentions context or suggests that the original language might offer additional insight, many will accuse them of "twisting" Scripture to their liking.

But context is never a threat. In fact, it's essential. If we don't contextualize the passages of Scripture applied to homosexuality, we run the risk of inserting our own cultural framework into the text, producing a meaning that sounds right to our own ears but is far afield of the author's intent.

It's easy to approach Scripture looking for tidy answers to the questions we ask today. We want to know: Is same-sex marriage biblical or not? I obviously have opinions about this, or I wouldn't be celibate, but that's not what this book is about. My goal isn't to convince you to affirm or condemn same-sex marriage. Instead, in the next few pages, I want to invite you into the complexity of a text that was *not* designed to answer this question in the first place. Instead of making the Bible "clear," I'm inviting you to embrace a Bible that is not always as "clear" as we'd like it to be.

The Limitations of Perspective

Contemporary discussions of the "clobber passages" (the infamous verses used to "clobber" LGBTQ people) focus almost exclusively on whether Paul was "clearly" condemning homosexuality in the New Testament. However, the lens through which this focus is possible—sexual orientation—did not exist until the nineteenth century. To approach the Bible by asking, "Is homosexuality clearly a sin?" is to approach it with an eisegetical lens from the outset.[1] The very nature of the question clouds our perspective.

Perhaps the most infamous clobber passage is 1 Corinthians 6:9–10. Let's consider the 1689 KJV translation: "Know ye not that the unrighteous shall not inherit the kingdom of God? Be not deceived: neither fornicators, nor idolaters, nor adulterers, *nor effeminate, nor abusers of themselves with mankind*, nor thieves, nor covetous, nor drunkards, nor revilers, nor extortioners, shall inherit the kingdom of God." According to this passage, the kingdom of God excludes the "effeminate" and "abusers of themselves with mankind."

But let's now consider the updated NKJV translation, which was published in 1982: "Do you not know that the unrighteous will not inherit the kingdom of God? Do not be deceived.

Neither fornicators, nor idolaters, nor adulterers, *nor homosexuals, nor sodomites,* nor thieves, nor covetous, nor drunkards, nor revilers, nor extortioners will inherit the kingdom of God." Here, the kingdom of God excludes "homosexuals" and "sodomites." What happened between 1689 and 1982? Why did the language shift so drastically?

The English word *effeminate* evokes a time when femininity occupied the lowest rung of the social ladder. We get the word *virtue* from the Latin word *virtus,* which comes from *vir,* meaning "man." To be masculine was to embody the *strength* of humanity in all of its glory. To be feminine was to embody the *weakness* of humanity in all of its vice. *Virtue* literally meant "manly" in ancient Rome.

Such is the origin of insults like "Don't be a sissy," or "You throw like a girl." "Being a man" is something we aspire to and "being a woman" is something we look down on. Calling someone a "girl" would have no power otherwise. In this sense, insulting a man by calling him a "woman" has less to do with femininity and more to do with negative associations attached to femininity. If you want to insult a man, for example, you compare him to a woman (sissy, pretty boy, girl, etc.), but if you want to insult a woman, you don't compare her to a man. In fact, saying she can do *x, y,* or *z* "like a man" is likely to be taken as a compliment. Instead, you call her an animal (bitch, heifer, pussy, etc.) or a sexual object (slut, whore, cunt, etc.).[2]

When we say the word *effeminate,* we can't help but think of women because "femininity" is embedded within the word itself. But this has less to do with any objective notion of femininity and more to do with the ways in which we unconsciously associate women with being "less than." "Femininity" is a useful insult to hurl at men because it's a useful insult to hurl at anyone.

Prior to the twentieth century, effeminacy did not strictly apply to men who engaged in same-sex behavior. The concept

91

referred to men who were "womanly" in the sense that they were weak, self-indulgent, and given to lust. Such men lacked control over their carnal desires, and literature often depicted effeminate men as besotted by love, typically for women. Consider the following excerpt from *Romeo and Juliet*, where Romeo bemoans his infatuation with Juliet's beauty.

> O sweet Juliet,
> Thy beauty hath made me effeminate,
> And in my temper softened valor's steel.[3]

Here, Romeo verbalizes the historic understanding of effeminacy that typically played out in what we might call "heterosexual" encounters today. Romeo became "effeminate" because Juliet's beauty exerted such power over him that it left him weak, "soft," overcome by her beauty when he ought to be girding for war. It was a product of carnal indulgence. Heterosexuality and homosexuality had nothing to do with it.

Nevertheless, ideas shifted following the development of psychopathology in the nineteenth century. Suddenly, men who experienced same-sex attraction were afflicted with a condition known as "homosexuality," wherein they matured like women instead of men. Clinicians pathologized male same-sex attraction as a symptom of "feminine" development, and in a relatively short amount of time, "effeminacy" became synonymous with "homosexuality." In 1946, the RSV became the first biblical translation to replace the word *effeminate* with *homosexual*. By the time the NKJV was published forty years later, the word *homosexual* was all but taken for granted in the passage.

Effeminacy in Scripture

This backdrop complicates modern interpretations of 1 Corinthians 6:9–10. In this passage, Christians commonly equate the "sin of softness" with "effeminacy," which, in turn, they assume to mean "homosexuality." The original Greek word, however, is *malakoi*. So what exactly does *malakoi* mean?

Malakos was common to the vocabulary of ancient Rome, but it only appears two other times in the New Testament. Its first appearance occurs in Matthew 11:8, where Jesus says to a crowd of onlookers, "What then did you go out to see? A man dressed in *soft* clothing? Behold, those who wear *soft* clothing are in kings' houses." The second appearance of *malakos* occurs in a retelling of the same story in Luke 7:25: "What then did you go out to see? A man dressed in *soft* clothing? Behold, those who are dressed in splendid clothing and live in luxury are in kings' courts."

In both passages, *malakos* refers to the "soft" clothing that only the wealthy can afford. Bibliographer Wayne Dynes describes the word as referring to "luxury, idleness, and pampered self-indulgence."[4] In Roman culture, "soft" men traded the "hard" virtues of masculinity, typically associated with war and battle, for the vices of so-called "womanly" passions, associated with enjoyment of wealth, food, leisure, and sex: "In the culture of the military elites of Europe, at least from the ancient world through the Renaissance, normative masculinity often entailed austerity, resistance to appetite, and mastery of the impulse to pleasure. . . . Men who refused to rise to the challenge, who abandoned the competitive society of men for the amorous society of women, who pursued a life of pleasure, who made love instead of war—they incarnated the classical stereotype of effeminacy."[5] Trading the "rational" world for the "impassioned" world defined ideas about "softness" or "effeminacy" from antiquity into the Renaissance (e.g., Juliet's beauty "softened" Romeo's "steel").

In ancient Rome, sexual conquest of "soft men" buttressed the masculinity of other men.[6] This might be confusing given that "soft men" pursued sexual encounters with women, but it goes hand in hand. In the context of Roman society, if you *only* had sex with women, it suggested a lack of masculinity. Unlike today, Roman masculinity had nothing to do with having "heterosexual" sex but, rather, with having *dominant* sex.[7] Raping other men functioned in a comparative way to express one man's superiority by raping another. "Except for some restraint to avoid conflict within his actual household," Classics scholar Sarah Ruden observes, "he positively strutted between his wife, his girlfriends, female slaves and prostitutes, and males. Penetration, after all, signaled moral uprightness. . . . In fact, society pressured a man into sexual brutality toward other males."[8]

Dominant males raped *malakoi* because raping inferior men was *expected* of masculinity.[9] *Malakoi*, in turn, were despised by Roman society because they were sexually conquered instead of sexually dominant. Over time, this culture evolved to a point where older men regularly kept younger men in their sexual entourage.

It Gets More Complicated

In addition to *malakoi*, debate over 1 Corinthians 6:9–10 centers on one additional word: *arsenokoitai*. The 1689 KJV translation renders this word "abusers of themselves with mankind." The 1982 NKJV later translated it as "sodomites." But if our exploration of *malakoi* is any indicator, the word *arsenokoitai* is a lot more complicated than most would assume.

The meaning of *arsenokoitai* is much less clear than *malakoi* because outside of Scripture it doesn't appear in ancient literature. Many biblical translators believe that *arsenokoitai* is a portmanteau of two words from Greek: *arsēn*, meaning "men," and *koitē*, meaning "bed." Translated literally, it means "men-bedders," and alongside *malakoi*, it means "soft men" and "men-bedders" will not inherit the kingdom of heaven.

However, scholars fiercely debate whether the two words—side by side—implicate consensual intercourse between members of the same sex or merely implicate rape and other forms of sexual conquest between men. Some argue that its placement alongside *malakoi* represents a double-edged condemnation of the *Roman* sexual system and does not apply to loving relationships. Others argue that these two words together condemn not only sexual exploitation between members of the same sex but also *loving* sexual relationships between members of the same sex.

Unlike most Christian books that engage LGBTQ issues, we're not going to spend significant time exploring this debate. Instead, I'd like to point out a more salient fact: the above debate is just that—a *debate*. There's nothing "clear" about it. In order to answer the questions raised, you'd have to know Greek and Hebrew—or find someone who does. Even then, scholars disagree on the correct interpretation given the historical context of the period, particularly considering the Roman gender hierarchy and the importance of sexual dominance. Ultimately, the only thing that ends up being "clear" is that it's a complicated conversation from start to finish, regardless of the conclusions we ultimately reach.

Many Christians balk at this. To them, everything *does* look clear. After all, they argue, 1 Corinthians 6:9 condemns *arsenokoitai*, which means "men who bed men." And "men who bed men" obviously refers to "homosexuals" and "homosexuality." But that's the thing. Not necessarily. As we saw in chapter 3, sexologists developed the concept of "homosexuality" to categorize the entire disposition of a person—their "orientation"—as a perversion. It was the product of pathological pseudoscience, and prior to the nineteenth century, the category didn't exist. In ancient Rome—where sexual attraction was peripheral to sexual dominance—the term would have been completely unintelligible. It would make about as much sense as inserting the words *Republican* and *Democrat* into the text, as though the modern two-party system in the US could accurately reflect the politics of ancient Rome.

Still, many Christians go to great lengths attempting to read the modern framework of sexual orientation into the pages of Scripture, pulling out arcane references to male desire from the peripheral margins of ancient literature to weave together a narrative that places the category of "homosexuality" into the context of ancient Israel and ultimately Rome.

The reality, however, is that ancient society had a different understanding of sexuality than modern Western culture has today. It was an expression of power, not attraction. Male penetration, in particular, was considered a virtue unto itself. People certainly experienced sexual attraction, but sexual attraction did not define human sexuality the way it does for society today. When translators force the category of "homosexuality" into the Bible, they effectively harness Scripture to reproduce a *modern* worldview.

Nevertheless, most modern English translations of the Bible use either *homosexual* or *homosexuality* despite the anachronism. Consider the 2001 ESV translation: "Or do you not know that the unrighteous will not inherit the kingdom of God? Do not be deceived: neither the sexually immoral, nor idolaters, nor adulterers, *nor men who practice homosexuality*, nor thieves, nor the greedy, nor drunkards, nor revilers, nor swindlers will inherit the kingdom of God."

Here, we see Paul's original language glossed over in its entirety and replaced by "men who practice homosexuality." Gone is any trace of the word *malakoi* and the complexities of its cultural baggage. Gone is any trace of *arsenokoitai* and the discomfort of dealing with a messy word. Instead, we have a nice and tidy condemnation of "men who practice homosexuality."

Many believe this translation to be an improvement because it distinguishes between *being* a "homosexual" and *practicing* "homosexuality." But what exactly does it mean to "practice homosexuality"? Christians typically build an entire system on this verse whereby *everything* about the gay experience—including same-sex attraction itself—is a sin that needs repentance.[10] Combined with other translations that reduce either *malakoi* or *arsenokoitai* to "homosexual," the damage is still immense. The result is a weapon that Christians easily wield to perpetuate psychopathological ideas—a "clear" condemnation of "homosexuality" that obscures the original language and disseminates Freudian psychology with the supposed backing of Scripture.

Grappling with Scripture

Even if you ultimately conclude—as I do—that the holistic teaching of Scripture supports a more traditional reading, the fact of the matter is that sexual orientation did not become attached to 1 Corinthians 6:9 (or other biblical passages) until *after* Freudian psychology became popular. Soon thereafter, many Christians developed an almost feverish commitment to maintaining the use of the term *homosexuality* in the Bible. From the perspective of LGBTQ people, it starts to look like many Christians are more committed to forcing Scripture to say "clearly" and explicitly that "homosexuality is a sin" than they are to understanding what Paul's words would have meant to a first-century audience.

The Roman understanding of gender and sexuality fueled a culture of sexual conquest, one where men existed at the top as human beings and women at the bottom as sexual objects. It was *this* culture that concerned Paul most, and it was *this* culture that he addressed, especially considering that the Corinthians had taken it to extremes that even most pagans wouldn't have (1 Cor. 5:1).

For this reason, only a few verses after the appearance of *malakoi* and *arsenokoitai*, Paul makes the following statement: "Each man should have his own wife and each woman her own husband. The husband should give to his wife her conjugal rights, and likewise the wife to her husband. For the wife does not have authority over her own body, but the husband does. Likewise the husband does not have authority over his own body, but the wife does" (1 Cor. 7:2b–4). It's difficult for modern readers to appreciate how revolutionary this statement would have been to the Corinthian church. In a culture where a man's very identity was wrapped up in a performance of sexual dominance, Paul comes around and dismantles the entire logic by which this culture operated. The "husband does not have authority over his own body, but the wife does"! Revolutionary barely scratches the surface.

However, in over three decades of listening to Sunday sermons week after week, I've yet to hear a single pastor discuss the implication of Paul's words in the context of his time. Sermons typically go from talking about "homosexuality" and "sexual perversion" in 1 Corinthians 6 to talking about how most people ought to get married—and quick—to avoid fornication in 1 Corinthians 7. The full weight of Paul's original point is lost, substituted for a modern replacement that barely does the job and does it poorly.

It's certainly okay to seek guidance from Scripture in discerning whether same-sex marriage is permissible—in fact it's necessary! But it's not okay to twist Scripture in order to artificially create "clarity" for a question that is actually complex. Insisting that the Bible is "clear" ultimately weakens the passage and causes readers to miss the original point.

Indeed, removing words like *homosexual* and *homosexuality* from the Bible makes people uncomfortable. It renders the question, "Does the Bible condemn gay sex?" a lot less apparent. Expending energy to prove that *homosexual* is a faithful translation of 1 Corinthians 6:9 is easier. After all, if the Bible explicitly says that "homosexuals" or "men who practice homosexuality" don't inherit the kingdom of God, the conversation is over.

But the fact of the matter is that the Bible doesn't explicitly say so. Is gay sex automatically okay as a result? Not necessarily. But it makes the conversation a lot messier. Suddenly, same-sex marriage requires the same careful and nuanced thinking that we apply to other difficult questions.

In my own experience, the Bible was only "clear" about homosexuality for as long as I was willing to never go beyond the surface. The minute I set aside my own worldview and studied the text in the context of its time, things got a lot more complicated. I realized that I couldn't rely on a verse here and a verse there to construct a biblical sexual ethic. I actually had to develop a holistic understanding of human sexuality given the full weight and breadth of God's Word. That takes time. It takes asking lots of questions and challenging the automatic answers we supply. It takes a willingness to not have solutions right away. To be okay with being unsure.

But for many people, this is too much to ask.

Consider Emily's story. She desperately needed someone to talk to. But the mere fact that she needed to talk was a sign of sin. Her parents took away her access to the outside world and kept her locked in their home for months until she found herself wanting to die—all because Emily was gay. She needed time to "process," as she put it, but there was no room for processing. In a world where the Bible is supposed to be "clear," Emily's very need to grapple with her faith and sexuality condemned her.

8. Double Standards

JONATHAN

Growing up in a Chinese-American family, Jonathan was accustomed to hearing white evangelical Christians criticize things about his culture. But Western gender roles in his white evangelical church felt just as arbitrary and just as driven by culture.

"Men are supposed to be the strong ones. We don't show emotions. We're expected to become the breadwinners in the family," Jonathan said of his American, Christian communities. Westernized conceptions at church layered atop the expectations of his family. "I was expected to make money so that my wife could stay home and take care of the kids. We'd buy a house and have this white-picket life, and it would all be great."

As a closeted gay teen, this vision of the good life felt impossible to achieve. Jonathan tried to imagine it, but he couldn't see living past thirty. "I knew I was attracted to men. I knew I was more emotional than other men. And I just knew this was going to get in the way of the plan that was written for my life."

He came out as gay to a mentor for the first time when he was sixteen, eventually coming out to others, but no one knew what to say. "Those were moments of complete desperation," he recalled. "I was about to physically harm myself. I felt like there was no reason for me to live my life."

In his twenties, the campus ministry that employed him started firing anyone who disagreed with their policies on same-sex marriage. Unsure of his own beliefs, he fell into a deep depression and started hiding in his bedroom, where he would sleep all day and contemplate the best way to end his life.

"It was impossible for me to be in process when I could literally be fired for coming to the wrong conclusion," Jonathan recalled. "I just needed space, but I had no permission to navigate theology or ask questions about same-sex marriage."

■ ■ ■

As a celibate lesbian, I'm stuck at an interesting intersection. On the one hand, many Christians question my faith or accuse me of sin just for being a lesbian. On the other hand, many use stories like mine as "proof" that other gay people ought to be celibate like me. Ironically, it's often the same people who do both. Curiously, in all the conversations I've had, I've rarely met a straight person who admonishes *themselves* to be celibate on account of my story. My celibacy is always a lesson to be given to the gays but not the straights.

I find this remarkable given the number of Christians who condemn homosexuality but also engage in contraceptive sex. A traditional reading of Scripture would condemn contraceptive sex just as strongly as gay sex. But if I mention this to heterosexual Christians, many take offense. To them, it sounds like I'm judging the private, personal decisions they make about their sex life. They feel like I'm saying they're living in sin just for having sex with someone they love. They believe it's none of my business what they choose to do in the privacy of their own bedroom, and they would like me to respect their Christian liberty and to worry about the sin in my own life, thank you very much. It reminds me of how gay people feel.

For most of Christian history up until a century ago, the Bible was just as "clear" on contraceptive sex as gay sex. In fact, most Christians believed contraception to be more serious than adultery and even akin to murder.[1] If you tried to say otherwise, you'd be considered a heretic. And lest you think it was merely a Catholic thing, it was in fact the near-unanimous opinion of all church scholars from the earliest days of Christianity up through the Protestant Reformation and into the 1920s.[2]

Contraceptive Sex

Much of the consensus rested on the "sin of Onan" described in Genesis 38:8–10. Here, Onan was legally obligated to "give offspring" to his dead brother's widowed wife, Tamar. Instead, however, he decided to "waste the semen on the ground" to prevent her from having children (v. 9). In the twentieth century, most Christians reinterpreted this passage to emphasize the illegality and selfishness of Onan's behavior. However, prior to the 1920s, Christians focused on the shocking nature of Onan's sexual conduct.[3] They understood the creation mandate ("be fruitful and multiply," Gen. 1:28) to be not only a positive commission but also an ethical restriction on the type of intercourse permitted within marriage. Onan, therefore, not only reneged on his legal duty. By intentionally subverting the procreative capacity of sex, he perverted the created order.

Most Christians believed that if Onan had only selfishly refused his legal duties, he wouldn't have died. After all, other men scoffed at the same legal duties and merely received a public shaming (Deut. 25:7–10). Scripture does not even record a punishment for Onan's younger brother, who never fulfilled his duty to Tamar even after coming of age (Gen. 38:14). Instead, Christians believed that Onan did something particularly heinous by "wasting the semen" during sexual intercourse (v. 9). It was this act of sexual perversion that warranted his death.

"Deliberately avoiding the intercourse," John Calvin said of Onan, "so that the seed drops on the ground, is double horrible.

For this means that one quenches the hope of his family, and kills the son . . . before he is born."[4] John Wesley likewise remarked that Onan disobeyed God "to the great abuse of his own body" and that those who follow his example "destroy their own souls."[5] Martin Luther observed that Onan deliberately subverted the "order of nature established by God in procreation."[6] "It is far more atrocious than incest and adultery," he said. "We call it unchastity, yes, a Sodomitic sin."[7]

Few would ever think sodomy applies to straight people today. Nowadays, most consider it a homosexual act and nothing else. But for most of Christian history, this distinction did not exist. The term applied to *all* non-procreative sex, whether heterosexual or homosexual, and it was considered a heinous crime however it was done. "We must condemn sodomy," remarked Clement of Alexandria, "*all* fruitless sowing of seed, *any* unnatural methods of holding intercourse and the reversal of the sexual role in intercourse."[8] "Pleasure sought for its own sake, even within the marriage bonds is a sin and contrary both to law and to reason."[9]

Other church fathers agreed. Married couples who resort to contraception, Augustine said, "although called by the name of spouses, are really not such; they retain no vestige of true matrimony, but pretend the honourable designation as a cloak for criminal conduct."[10] "Some go so far as to take potions," said Jerome, "that they may insure barrenness, and thus murder human beings almost before their conception."[11] "In performing their filthy act either with men or with women they forbear insemination," Epiphanius said, "rendering impossible the procreation God has given his creatures—as the apostle says, 'receiving in themselves the recompense of their error which was meet.'"[12]

Here, Epiphanius is quoting Romans 1:27, where Paul says that they received "in themselves the due penalty for their error." Today, this passage is typically understood as a condemnation of homosexuality, but Epiphanius—and his contemporaries—understood Romans 1:27 to condemn not homosexuality but rather *nonprocreative* sex. It wasn't the fact that two men or two women were having sex that horrified early Christians. Rather, it was the fact that they subverted procreation. St. Clement references the "unnatural lusts" of Romans 1:27 in concluding that "pleasure sought for its own sake, *even within the marriage bonds*, is a sin and contrary both to law and to reason."[13]

Ironically, many heterosexual Christians like to quote Romans 1:27 to condemn gay people. However, a traditional reading of the passage likely condemns their own lifestyle as well.

The Social Construction of Clarity

My point is not to argue that most heterosexual couples in the church are unrepentant sodomites. If you are among the vast majority of sexually active heterosexual Christians in the church, you likely use contraceptives.[14] I'm certainly not trying to accuse you of sin. I do have a few married friends who abstain from contraceptive sex due to their traditional beliefs. As a result, they are celibate unless they want to have kids.[15] However, I don't look at these friends as somehow "holier" than my friends who engage in contraceptive sex. In the context of modern society, the ethical questions raised by contraception are complex and often confusing, and I believe it's important to give couples grace in how they navigate those questions.

In other words, I'm not trying to condemn people. Instead, my point is to consider the contradiction. Why is it that, in barely a paragraph above, I can so casually say that these types of heterosexual questions are "complex," but it takes an entire book to say the same exact thing about LGBTQ issues? Why am I unlikely to be called a heretic for giving straight Christians permission to essentially ignore two millennia of near-unanimous church teaching on sexual ethics, but if I do the same thing for gay people, I'm likely to be tarred and feathered?

The response goes something like this: *You can't compare contraceptive sex to gay sex. The Bible is clear on homosexuality. No such clarity exists for things like contraception. Contraception is obviously a disputable matter whereas homosexuality is clearly condemned.*

However, "biblical clarity" doesn't always mean what many Christians think it does. More often than not, clarity tells us more about our own cultural biases and presuppositions than it does about God's Word. Indeed, this whole debate about contraceptive sex was not even disputable for most theologians historically. The procreative restrictions of the creation mandate were "clear" and the punishment for subverting this mandate equally explicit. How is it that heterosexual Christians today legitimately believe they've somehow discovered a groundbreaking new heterosexual truth that was otherwise unknown to the Christian church prior to the twentieth century?

Most Christians are accustomed to asking this type of question about gay people, not themselves. Reversing the question draws a striking parallel. Many say that condemnations of contraceptive sex rely on a misreading of the "sin of Onan" and a Draconian interpretation of the creation mandate. Interestingly, many gay Christians likewise say that condemnations of homosexuality rely on a misreading of a few verses and a similarly Draconian interpretation of the creation mandate.

Other Christians say that ancient people mistakenly believed that male semen contained the "seed" of a human being, causing them to conclude that "wasting the semen" was murder. With scientific advancements, they say, we now know that semen must fertilize an egg first in order to conceive. Curiously, many gay Christians likewise argue that ancient people didn't understand sexual attraction. With scientific advancements, they say, we now know that some people are naturally attracted to the same sex.

Still other Christians say that it's wrong to compare gay sex to contraceptive sex because sex between two men or two women is "unnatural" whereas sex between a husband and wife reflects the created order (Rom. 1:27). However, if contraceptive sex is perfectly "natural," it's a bit unclear just what exactly Christians mean when they talk about the "created order." If gay people are doing something unnatural in subverting the purpose of sex, why aren't straight people doing something unnatural when they, too, subvert the purpose of sex? It starts to sound like many Christians define the word *natural* as merely *heterosexual* instead of by submitting to God's design.

Who Gets to Be Normal?

Most people don't listen to someone debate the merits of having contraceptive sex with their spouse and say, "What's next? Sex with donkeys and monkeys?" Most people don't listen to someone debate the merits of getting remarried after a divorce and say, "If we let this happen, incest and pedophilia are just around the bend!"

The reason is that people tend to see their own experiences as relatable, understandable, and the way things "ought" to be regardless of whether those experiences are universal. When people ask a question that we ourselves have asked, we see it as "normal." But when people ask a question that challenges the bounds of our limited existence, we see it as a "threat."

The result is that many Christians hold a strict standard when it comes to homosexuality but ask for grace when it comes to matters affecting heterosexuality. My point is *not* to say that most heterosexual believers are a bunch of sodomites. Instead, my point is to expose a double standard. Many people balk at

LGBTQ believers who seem to "explain away" certain proof-texts in their embrace of same-sex marriage. But proof-texting has not applied to heterosexual questions about sex and marriage for a very long time.

Many LGBTQ people observe that Christians would never *dream* of approaching questions about cisgender heterosexuality in the same way they approach questions about LGBTQ issues. Queer people could easily proof-text their way to showing that the Bible condemns not only contraceptive sex but also divorce and remarriage. They too would have the full weight of Christian history and tradition on their side. But I've never seen a straight Christian annul their second marriage and commit to a life of celibacy based on this logic. Such people surely exist, but they would be the exception in evangelical communities that broadly accept divorce and remarriage as normal.

On the topic of divorce and remarriage, John Piper is among the few attempting consistency. He engages each of the main biblical passages on divorce and concludes that the Bible prohibits "all remarriage except in the case where a spouse has died."[16] Prior to modernity, the vast majority of Christians would agree.[17] This is part of what made the Christian ethic revolutionary in the context of ancient Rome, where divorce and remarriage were rampant.

Consider Matthew 19:9, which says that "whoever divorces his wife, except for sexual immorality, and marries another, commits adultery." Modern readers reinterpret this passage as a license to get divorced on the grounds of "sexual immorality." But the vast majority of Christian writers for the first fifteen hundred years of church history believed the opposite.[18] As Piper explains, the early church understood Jesus to be saying that sexual immorality *prior* to consummating the marriage was the only grounds for divorce, given that the vows were not yet consummated.[19] Today's reading—permitting divorce *after* consummation—only arose to prominence in the modern era.

A closer look at Piper's perspective illuminates something else: Christians like to settle debates over marriage by making room for disagreement. Piper concludes that *all* remarriage is *adulterous* unless the previous spouse is dead but nevertheless recommends that pastors give grace for Christians to differ. "Every person and church," he says, "must teach and live according to the dictates of its own *conscience* informed by a serious study of Scripture."[20] The official statement of Piper's church further recognizes that "complete unanimity does not exist" concerning divorce and remarriage and makes room for differences of belief.[21]

How could Piper conclude that all remarriage is *adulterous* apart from the death of the previous spouse but also make room for Christians to differ? Wouldn't he be making a concession to sin? How is he not giving adulterers a free pass? Curiously, when examined apart from LGBTQ issues, most Christians see no contradiction. They recognize that divorce and remarriage are complicated. Consensus might have existed in the past, but in a complex world, we need to give people grace, not legalism.

It's worth noting that many fundamentalist churches do take a more militant position, shaming Christians who get divorced and forcing them to remain celibate unless they remarry their original spouse. In some situations, women are pressured to remain with abusive husbands. Nevertheless, the dominant perspective within evangelicalism, and Western Protestantism more broadly, rejects this type of thinking. Even most who maintain a traditional perspective would never tell a divorced person to be celibate for the rest of their life. Nor would they tell a remarried person that they're living in adultery.

Similar themes emerge with contraceptive sex. A vocal minority of fundamentalist churches *do* take a militant approach to contraception, going so far as to deny women access to birth control.[22] The undue burden such approaches place on cisgender women and anyone assigned female at birth (AFAB) is extreme, robbing them of the ability to make decisions about pregnancy and significantly impacting a host of other health concerns for which birth control is necessary. Once again, however, the majority of conservative evangelicals and even lay Catholics reject this approach. Most believe that women ought to have freedom to follow their conscience when it comes to birth control, and most couples embrace contraception.[23]

At this point, you might be thinking, "So what? Just because Sally gets to do something doesn't mean that Suzy can too." And I agree. Just because most Christians accept modern reinterpretations of Scripture that impact straight people doesn't mean that modern reinterpretations of Scripture that impact gay people are necessarily okay. But remember, this book isn't about convincing readers to affirm or condemn same-sex marriage. Instead, this book is about people and how we treat them. If Sally makes a mistake and I tell her, "Aw, that's okay, sweetie. Everybody makes mistakes. It's part of growing up!" but Suzy makes the same mistake and I tell her, "Go to your bedroom, you selfish brat," it's pretty clear that the problem is not Suzy's behavior but rather my favoritism.

Consider Jonathan's experience. His Christian employer gave an ultimatum: agree with our theology about same-sex marriage or you're fired. Jonathan didn't even know what he believed yet, but with such severe repercussions for potentially disagreeing with his employer, he had no space to grow and learn. His employer didn't release any kind of similar ultimatum for cisgender heterosexuality, whether about divorce and remarriage or contraceptive sex.

Straight people get the grace. Gay people get the legalism.

BURDEN 4 SUMMARY

We thus conclude the fourth burden that LGBTQ Christians bear in the church. Most heterosexual Christians believe the Bible to be incredibly complex when it comes to questions that they themselves ask about traditional teaching. But when it comes to LGBTQ issues, the Bible is suddenly "clear." No questions. No thinking. End of story.

BURDEN 5

"REAL" MEN, "GOOD" LADIES

9. Effeminacy

BRYAN

Bryan had never told anyone that he was gay. But somehow the boys at school just knew. One group, an athletics club for Christian teens, bullied him relentlessly.

"They'd write things on my locker," Bryan recalled. "They'd come by and egg my house, punch me at school."

Another boy named Elijah was bullied for being bisexual. One day, Bryan couldn't take it anymore and told the teens to back down. Not willing to lose a fight, the club president got his friends together during lunch, dragged Bryan and Elijah outside, tied them both to a tree in the center of an open quad, and beat them nearly unconscious. Inscribed across their foreheads: the word *fag*.

"I still don't remember the actual physical hits," Bryan told me. "I just remember cleaning up the blood off myself. Sometimes, when I sleep at night or close my eyes or think about it, like I'm doing now, I can feel the blows coming toward me."

Bryan moved and started going to a new school and a new church. But the teens at youth group noticed Bryan's "effeminacy" and decided they needed to "toughen him up." Over the next year, Bryan found himself subjected to beatings outside the church's youth center, sometimes multiple times a week.

"They would try to get me to punch or fight them," Bryan said. "They'd walk up to me, punch me square in the face and be like, 'Fight back! Fight back!'" When he didn't fight back, they'd push him down and kick him repeatedly, sometimes in the presence of adults. "They thought they could butch me up," Bryan said. "You know, make me what I was supposed to be."

At one point in high school, Bryan got in touch with a man who offered to help him sort through his questions about sexuality. "How do you know when you're gay?" Bryan remembered asking.

The man convinced Bryan to pick him up so they could drive together. "I was like, okay. I'll pick you up in my truck and then we can head over to get coffee," Bryan recalled. "So I knocked on his door . . . and then . . ." The man overpowered Bryan and raped him.

Bryan went home that day utterly destroyed and unable to make sense out of what happened. Eventually, he told his mom. But when she found out, she couldn't accept that her son was gay. She gave him thirty minutes to pack up his things and leave the house. So Bryan left at the age of seventeen and started living out of his truck.

"At the time, I didn't think I could be Christian and gay," Bryan told me. "You had to choose." He kept a shotgun in the back of his truck. Evening came at the end of a long week, and he made a decision. "I took what little money I had left, and I bought the ammunition to kill myself."

■ ■ ■

Vasco Nuñez de Balboa was the first European to reach the Pacific Ocean by way of the Americas, claiming its shores for God and country. Like many Europeans of the sixteenth century, including the French and British in North America, Balboa was horrified by what he described as rampant effeminacy in the Native men. Upon finding one tribe to be "infected with the most abominable and unnaturall lechery," where the Indigenous king's brother and a host of young men dressed in "women's apprarell, smoth & effeminately decked," he rounded up about forty of these "effeminate" men, stripped them naked, and unleashed on them a pack of ravenous dogs that tore them limb from limb.[1]

A 1590 engraving of the massacre depicts bloodied bodies, severed heads, and ferocious dogs sinking teeth into terrified faces as a group of European men—flamboyantly dressed in tassels, ribbons, and embroidery, hips daintily cocked to one side—stand watch. The rest of the tribe gave "tokens" to God in repentance and converted to Christianity.[2]

History is filled with stories of Christian colonizers enacting harsh and often murderous punishment on "savages" whom they believed to be violating gender.[3] Five hundred years later, concepts of effeminacy and emasculation continue to shape how Christians think about gender.

The Dominance Paradigm Today

In college, my friends and I would often talk about masculinity. All of us were conservative-minded believers interested in "biblical manhood and womanhood," but masculinity was hard to pin down. "Perfect strength under perfect control" was our favorite definition, culled from the available literature on biblical manhood. We'd talk about what it meant to be a "real man," and for some reason our voices would deepen, our brows furrow, and our bodies tense up whenever we said it. Upon closer inspection, our thoughts about "real men" looked surprisingly similar to the ancient Roman paradigm.

Indeed, the lasting influence of Roman culture means that ancient pagan assumptions continue to shape Western masculinity, infiltrating how we think, talk, and behave in ways we don't even see. Roman culture invented the "strength under control" motif, believing self-control to be central to masculinity. Real men not only controlled their passions. They knew how to direct their passions toward virtuous ends.[4] They were fearless warriors who conquered their appetites as well as their foes and safeguarded the weak and vulnerable. Western notions about chivalry trace much of their ancestry to such ideals.[5]

What's so wrong with being a fearless warrior? Assuming we mean the type of warrior who fights for justice and defends the helpless, the answer is nothing. We need those people! The Roman mistake was in the conflation of virtue with manliness and in the elevation of power as the end of manliness. Cultural ideas about masculinity came to define virtue instead of *virtue* defining how men ought to live.

In Western churches, the pagan elevation of strength, aggression, and dominance as the ultimate end of masculinity continues to haunt Christian men. Consider the following excerpt from the classic text on biblical manhood, John Eldredge's *Wild at Heart*, which sold over four million copies in the US alone:

> Little girls do not invent games where large numbers of people die, where bloodshed is a prerequisite for having fun. Hockey, for example, was not a feminine creation. Nor was boxing. A boy wants to attack something—and so does a man even if it's only a little white ball on a tee. He wants to whack it into kingdom come. On the other hand, my boys do not sit down to tea parties. They do not call their friends on the phone to talk about relationships. They grow bored of games that have no element of danger or competition or bloodshed. Cooperative games based on 'relational interdependence' are complete nonsense. 'No one is killed?' they ask, incredulous. 'No one wins? What's the point?' The universal nature of this ought to have convinced us by now: The boy is a warrior; the boy is his name.[6]

Eldredge later describes a time when one of his sons gave him a bloody lip in a wrestling match. He explains, with pride, that this display of aggression was a sign that his little boy was growing up. He "shook his antlers at me," Eldredge remarks.[7] The message of the book is that every man has three core desires "deep down" in his heart: "a battle to fight, an adventure to live, and a beauty to rescue."[8]

Eldredge articulates a type of "heroic aggression" espoused by some of the most influential Christian ministries today. In *Raising a Modern-Day Knight*, a best-selling book published by Focus on the Family, Robert Lewis relies almost entirely on Western chivalry in his depictions of biblical manhood.[9] In another best-selling book, *The Tender Warrior*, Stu Weber similarly relies on a benevolent-aggressor archetype—the man-as-tender-warrior—to develop his conception of a man who is "every woman's dream" and "every child's hope."[10] Writing in 2019 for the Council on Biblical Manhood and Womanhood (CBMW), Colin Smothers argues that to "describe 'power, dominance, and aggression' as male is nearly a tautology. Replacing these *in toto* would be to replace men."[11]

The message is that real men model Christlikeness by being warriors who direct their aggression toward virtuous ends, such as protecting women and children. To borrow the language of a popular father-son event, real men are "born to be brave."[12]

Of course, there's nothing necessarily wrong with being a "tender warrior," but we run into problems when Christians universalize this Western construct, defining the measure of a man based on his proximity to this ideal. Many if not most of the texts on biblical manhood *do* contain valuable insights from Scripture. The problem is not the Scripture they use but the cultural manifestations that many depict, celebrate, and ultimately universalize. Behind every exhortation for men to be "more like Christ" is an incarnation of this precept that evokes images of battle. Behind every reference to humility is an example of tenderness that preserves the man's power—the daring prince who rescues the lady in waiting. The heroic knight in shining armor. Compassionate aggressor. Benevolent boss.

Christian masculinity thereby comes to be defined by a man's ability to assert power in virtuous ways, often couched in the language of headship. While there's nothing wrong with being a powerful man, problems emerge when power defines masculinity. At the end of the day, not every man is a knight in shining armor. What if "tough and tender" doesn't describe you as well as something like "gracious and eloquent" or "kind and sweet" or even "meek and mild"? Is there space for you to be a "real" man in such a universe?

Too often the answer is no.

The Ones Who Don't Fit

Most Christian writers who talk about the "sin of effeminacy" acknowledge the dual danger of brutish aggression, on the one hand, or floppy softness, on the other. "Real men," they say, find the mean between extremes.

Even so, most nevertheless conflate the "sin of softness" with being a woman. In that sense, the "extremes" that a man must battle view femininity itself as a vice. Femininity comes to be defined by whatever the majority culture deems to be weak and passive. As a result, anything that a majority of women tend to do, say, or like that can't be reasonably translated into "genteel taste" (e.g., going to the ballet is fine, but hosting a cupcake party is not) defines the sin of "softness."

Such logic encourages men to prove their masculinity through ever grander displays of their own superiority to avoid accusations of effeminacy. Concepts of "effeminacy," however, receive no legitimate definition beyond "the things women do," which is code for "the things men deem to be beneath themselves." In a culture that pathologizes deviance, this logic collapses into prejudice against queer men perceived to be "effeminate." "Effeminacy" meanwhile bears no resemblance to objective ideas about femininity but, instead, reflects the arbitrary expectations of a fallen culture.

In criticizing a Gillette commercial that took aim at toxic masculinity, for example, an article published by Desiring God decried the "sin of effeminacy" by relying almost entirely on gay stereotypes: "Just having returned from [a vacation to Orlando], my wife and I were shocked at how many men boldly acted like women. Lispy sentences, light gestures, soft mannerisms, and flamboyant jokes were everywhere to be seen—on display for a park flooded with children. No hiding it. No shame. No apologizing. This perversion of masculinity warranted no commercials."[13]

In a follow-up article, the author, Greg Morse, suggests that "effeminate" qualities are a sign of damnation.[14] He condemns the "gay vibe" and questions not only the masculinity but also the salvation of men who wear "floral shirts and tight jeans." He avoids specifically defining the sin of effeminacy, suggesting instead that effeminacy is an "obvious forest to all honest men and women."[15] Effeminate men, Morse says, drink "nonfat lattes" instead of black coffee. They wield a "plastic fork" instead of a sword.[16] And as the follow-up article suggests, they go to hell instead of heaven.[17]

Reliance on the so-called obvious pervades Christian writing about gender. In a 2012 article, for example, Kevin DeYoung names what he considers to be "obvious examples" of activities that are off-limits to "real" men: "Can real men enjoy musical theater and ballet and fine clothing? Surely they can and do. But on the other hand, if you met a guy who told you his favorite thing in the whole world was shopping for shoes, his favorite show was *Say Yes to the Dress*, and he got most of his news from *The View*, you'd be right to be concerned."[18]

Even though some people might consider *The View* to be tacky television, it's unclear how DeYoung's "obvious examples" legitimately subvert masculinity in any objective sense. He largely relies on arbitrary associations to make inherently subjective claims. While some readers might not entirely care for shows like *Say Yes to the Dress* or *The View*, inscribing such opinions into the definition of masculinity, simply because a good number of women enjoy those shows, is far afield of Scripture.

Like many, DeYoung defends this perspective using Paul's injunction to "act like men" in 1 Corinthians 16:13. However, given that Paul exhorts the Corinthians to put away their "childish ways," it's unlikely that Paul meant "stop watching *The View*, because it's mostly women who enjoy that sort of television." "When I was a child," Paul says, "I spoke like a child, I thought like a child, I reasoned like a child. When I became a man, I gave up childish ways" (1 Cor. 13:11). In the next chapter, Paul says, "Brothers, do not be children in your thinking" (14:20). Paul's letter communicates a plea for the Corinthians to "grow up." In this context, it makes little sense to construct a paradigm for effeminacy based on the exhortation to "act like men."

Curiously, most writing on biblical manhood and womanhood acknowledges the arbitrary nature of concepts like effeminacy. But whereas Christians typically see fallen culture as needing transformation, most biblical manhood and womanhood writers see culture to be largely *determinative* of Christian ideas about gender. Of course, there's nothing inherently wrong with cultural norms. Culture is a good thing! But culture, like everything else in the world, is also fallen. When we rely on culture to define our understanding of human identity, we make ourselves the definers of truth. "Fitting in" to fallen cultural norms erroneously becomes a biblical yardstick.

Consider the following passage from *Recovering Biblical Manhood and Womanhood*: "Every culture has different sets of behaviors that are arbitrarily classified as masculine or feminine. . . . There is nothing wrong with this if these arbitrary categories do not interfere with the freedom of individuals of both sexes to develop their potential competencies. As long as the arbitrary social labels of 'for men only' or 'for women only' do not hinder freedom to use one's talents, then they are benign or harmless sex-role stereotypes."[19] Here, psychologist and Southern Baptist minister George Alan Rekers acknowledges the arbitrary nature of many gender norms. He even suggests that such norms are good only insofar as they don't inhibit a person's "potential competencies." He goes on to name things like lipstick, nail polish, and certain clothing and hair styles—citing each as an example of arbitrary "sex-role stereotypes."[20]

Nevertheless, following this admission, he tells parents they *must* teach these arbitrary norms to children, especially if their children struggle to comply. Might their struggle be a sign that arbitrary "sex-role stereotypes" are not always good for every child? Aside from obvious statements like boys shouldn't be chauvinistic and girls shouldn't be forced to play the nurse in pretend games of hospital, the author says little. Instead, he argues that if parents fail to teach sex-role stereotypes to their children, their children may never develop a proper male and female "identity."[21] He acknowledges that "sex-role stereotypes" are arbitrary, culturally defined, and even potentially harmful, but he tells parents that such stereotypes are essential to their children's identity regardless.[22]

The result of such teaching is predictable. Too often, Christian ministries approach masculinity in such a way that cultural norms rise to the status of gospel necessity. Christians learn that God requires a certain type of man and *only that* type of man. Teachers will criticize the dangers of macho masculinity but nevertheless create the conditions where macho men are the only type of men allowed to exist.

Consider Bryan's experience. The teens from his youth group sniffed out his "effeminate" tendencies and decided to "man him up." This meant violently beating him multiple times a week outside their church's youth center—sometimes in the presence of adults who did nothing to stop them. The boys said Bryan needed to learn to "fight back." But why? Bryan told me it felt wrong to fight back given the example of Jesus who turned the other cheek. But neither the boys at youth group nor the adults at church seemed to value this version of masculinity.

10. Emasculation

HANNAH

Hannah grew up in an evangelical homeschool community and attended a Reformed church. There, she learned that "men and women are very different and complete each other. Men are aggressive and heroic. Women are nurturing." But the expectations didn't always make sense.

"My dad and I would go shooting together. We'd ride ATVs and go camping," she recalled. "But then my dad didn't want me driving the manual transmission because I'm a girl. . . . It was just really odd because I was allowed to be a tomboy for some things but then for other things I wasn't."

At one point, Hannah's mother fell ill and was unable to function for months at a time, but her father refused to step up to fill the gap in household chores. As the eldest of three, Hannah found herself cooking and cleaning and doing the laundry for the whole family. "Men are the breadwinners, and women the homemakers," she explained to me.

Hannah eventually attended a Christian college where she worked on campus. A few months into the first semester, her boss started making sexual advances. At first it was "accidental" touches. Then he started talking about his penis and bragging about the girls he had slept with. Then he suggested that he was regularly masturbating to pictures of her.

Hannah eventually got up the courage to report him, and enough evidence emerged that he was fired. But then a replacement arrived, and the new boss was just as bad as the last. Soon, the harassment started all over again.

"I started planning my trips so that he'd miss the elevator by the time the door closed. I'd hold my breath and pray, 'Please, God, please don't let him get on with me.'"

Worried that people might think she was lying or at fault, Hannah never reported his behavior. She had already reported her last boss. Would people take her seriously a second time? It took other women submitting multiple reports over the span of a year to finally get him fired.

"I had done nothing to deserve being sexually harassed for two years, but I still struggled with the idea that I might be responsible for what happened," Hannah said. "A friend of mine had to tell me every day for a full year that it wasn't my fault before I finally started to believe it."

MEREDITH

As a child, riding a dirt bike and rolling around in the grass was much more interesting to Meredith than playing with Barbies. Her mother put her in dresses and pretty shoes, but a skinned knee inevitably lurked underneath.

When she was six, her mother tried explaining to her how babies are made, pointing to pictures in the *Encyclopedia Britannica*. "When a man and woman love each other, they have sex. The penis goes into the vagina. Sperm fertilizes an egg; and then nine months later a baby is born. Do you have any questions?" Meredith wanted to go back to playing with her Erector Set.

But as she got older, sexuality played an increasingly restrictive role in her life, heightened by her status as a Black woman. "Men are going to look at you like you're a grown woman," her mother warned. "They're not going to realize that you're a little girl. You have to be careful not to tantalize men."

At the time, Meredith sported ripped jeans, T-shirts, and short-cropped hair. As she developed an awareness of her own sexuality and learned that she was queer, she realized that her obliviousness to men stemmed from not caring about most men in the first place. And yet Meredith's life increasingly became a maze of navigating various "don'ts": "Don't act like this. Don't walk like so. Don't dress like that." Somehow her life still revolved around men.

"It was confusing, scary, and shameful," Meredith recalled. Even when she started dating her future husband, people saw her as just fulfilling a sexual fantasy for her white male partner. After they got married, many would act surprised if she ever paid for meals at restaurants or ordered for the both of them.

Meredith loved being a woman, but as a queer Black woman, not everything about her life was "feminine" the way Christians expected. She liked to build things and fix stuff. She was a successful professional, in charge of managing others, and asserted herself when necessary in social situations.

Then again, neither was her husband "masculine" in the way Christians expected. He liked to cook, and at certain points in their relationship, Meredith's income surpassed his. It worked for them. They loved each other, and they fit. And yet Meredith couldn't help but feel keenly aware of how she failed to live up to the expectations of white evangelical culture.

"I never felt like I could be authentically myself. I had to be somehow strong and quiet at the same time. Dress femininely but not provocatively. Have a husband and bear children, because that's what you're supposed to do." When she discovered she couldn't bear children, biblical womanhood felt farther away than ever. Getting pregnant was the one thing she could still do to live up to the role that Christians had told her to play. Now she couldn't do even that.

"To be a true woman was to be a doting, submissive homemaker," Meredith said. "And anything less than that was not enough. That's what I learned from the church."

■ ■ ■

When fallen culture measures masculinity through expressions of power and dominance, the resulting prejudice against so-called limp-wristed men for being effeminate makes sense. But when we consider women, it gets confusing. "Effeminate" men are sinful, but "tomboy" girls are athletic. Men who wear makeup and nail polish are "homos," but women who hunt and shoot guns are sexy. Men can't wear dresses nearly a century after women donned pants.

It looks contradictory, but in fact, it makes sense. If femininity is an inferior expression of humanity, then a man *debases* himself by engaging in the activities that mostly women do. On the other hand, if masculinity is a superior expression of humanity, then a woman *elevates* herself by engaging in the activities that mostly *men* do.

In many Christian contexts, this means that women are allowed to enter the male arena as long as they defer to male authority. Women learn to see femininity as bearing all the same potentialities as masculinity, provided they stay in their place. A woman's place, in this context, means affirming the superiority of the men God puts in her life. Women can wear pants as long as they don't cause men to stumble. They can get a job as long as their husband is the breadwinner. They can serve in the church as long as they don't have authority. Where masculinity is defined by the exercise of power, femininity is defined by submission to power.

In *Set-Apart Femininity*, best-selling author Leslie Ludy writes that Christ transforms every woman into a "radiant, victorious, world-changing, set-apart young woman."[1] Stories of heroic women doing extraordinary things in their pursuit of God's kingdom fill the pages of every chapter. God's sacred call for women, she says, is "absolute abandonment to Jesus Christ, entire separation from the pollution of the world, and ardent worship of our King with every breath we take."[2]

Interestingly, however, Ludy's descriptions could also be true of men—and *should* be true of men. Among many stories and reflections, *submission* is the *only* spiritual quality that applies to women alone.

Nancy Leigh DeMoss's writing in *Becoming God's True Woman* reflects the same problem. Here DeMoss provides a comprehensive list of qualities that ought to characterize a "true woman." Among the qualities she names—pure in heart, chosen by God, available to God, believing God, praising God, trusting God, studying his Word, humble, influential, praying, devoted, Spirit-filled—all of them could also reflect the qualities of a Christian man. The only thing that distinguishes her "portrait of a true woman" from a similar "portrait of a true man" is submission.[3] In the same book, Carolyn Mahaney says that even *single* women must fulfill their femininity by submitting to men: "There are men in your life that the Lord has provided in this season—fathers, bosses, friends—and they need to know that you 'incline' toward them, instead of resisting them in a stiff-necked posture of the heart. You encourage their godly leadership when you seek their counsel before making your own decisions. You respect them when you avoid sinfully complaining to others about their actions or decisions and resist publicly questioning their actions."[4] The implication is that fulfilling God's calling for womanhood depends on one's ability to affirm male authority, regardless of your life situation.

Emasculation

Concepts of "emasculation" emerge whenever women fail to support, affirm, or buoy male power. Where effeminacy reveals how culture punishes men for engaging in behavior deemed *beneath* their masculinity, emasculation reveals how culture punishes women for engaging in behavior deemed *above* their femininity.

Consider the best-selling book on Christian femininity *Captivating: Unveiling the Mystery of a Woman's Soul*. Here, John and Stasi Eldredge say that women "pretty much fall into one of three categories: Dominating Women, Desolate Women, or Arousing Women." Dominating women "emasculate" men by not *needing* men, they argue. Desolate women "emasculate" men by not *stimulating* men. The *only* godly woman is an "arousing woman." Arousal, they explain, refers not only to sexual arousal between husband and wife but also to the many ways in which a man needs his masculinity to be affirmed or, as they put it, "aroused" by women.[5]

Like its predecessor (*Wild at Heart*), *Captivating* sold millions of copies worldwide when it was published in 2005, launching Bible studies, a guided journal, and a Christian video series.[6] Despite its popularity—or perhaps *because* of it—*Captivating* exposes a concerning mindset. No chapter defines men by their ability to "arouse" women in the Eldredge's companion book on masculinity. Finding a "beauty to rescue" is just one facet of the man's "wild" life with God. Women, however, need to be romanced by a *man*, participate in a *man's* adventure, and unveil their beauty to a *man*. While masculinity is a good thing in and of itself, femininity is a good thing only insofar as it exists to affirm masculinity. Where men have the full breadth of their God-given potential spread out before them, women have the full breadth of their God-given potential spread out before them to be realized only insofar as men are in charge.

Consequently, the most common and widely accepted Christian definition of gender reproduces a paradigm where the only definitive difference between men and women is the power dynamic between them. Consider the following definitions of masculinity and femininity written by John Piper and published by the Council on Biblical Manhood and Womanhood:

> At the heart of mature masculinity is a sense of benevolent responsibility to lead, provide for and protect women in ways appropriate to a man's differing relationships.

At the heart of mature femininity is a freeing disposition to affirm, receive and nurture strength and leadership from worthy
men in ways appropriate to a woman's differing relationships.[7]

In other words, men are leaders, providers, and protectors.
Women are the people men lead, provide, and protect. Men
are in charge, and women their charges.

Piper qualifies both definitions by admitting their limitations. "The definitions are not exhaustive," he says, "but they
touch all of us. They are an attempt to get at the heart, or at
least an indispensable aspect, of manhood and womanhood."[8]

However, the entire book nevertheless depends exclusively
on these two definitions in order to extrapolate how men and
women ought to live. Every treatment of Scripture, including
every answer to every question, goes through *this* paradigm
first. Piper's definitions effectively drive the conclusions, which
are themselves reproductions of the definitions.

Thirty years later, the most pervasive Christian approaches
to gender still can't identify any additional "indispensable aspects" of manhood and womanhood that don't ultimately reduce to male power. Aimee Byrd observes that this inevitably
leads to ridiculous scenarios in teaching from the Council on
Biblical Manhood and Womanhood. A mailman comes to the
door, but a woman answers. He must therefore consider how
to interact in a way that affirms his leadership. A man gets lost
and the only available person to give directions is a woman. He
must therefore consider how to ask for directions in a way that
doesn't compromise his authority.[9]

Growing up in a conservative evangelical context, I struggled
to find any resource on biblical femininity where the only difference between men and women was *not* a power dynamic.
In college, I studied book after book on biblical womanhood.
I invited a prominent female speaker to my campus to speak,
and I bookmarked every article I could find online. Time and

again, being a "godly woman" looked identical to being a good and faithful Christian—until I got to submission. I realized these books, articles, and speakers couldn't articulate the differences between men and women in any developed way *apart* from submission. Where dominance defined men, submission defined women.

Not surprisingly, the result is a culture that encourages abusive power dynamics to go unreported. Godly women are supposed to "respect" men by not "sinfully complaining to others about their actions or decisions" or "publicly questioning their actions."[10] Abused women must therefore weigh their need for safety against the social cost of usurping male authority. Often they're made to feel responsible for the man's abusive behavior. Worse, should they speak up, the man is more likely to be believed by virtue of his higher status in the first place.

Among the most recent examples of this is Ravi Zacharias, who used his position as an influential Christian leader to sexually abuse hundreds of women during his time in ministry. Zacharias died an esteemed and celebrated Christian evangelist, but behind closed doors he spent most of his career soliciting sexual favors from women under his influence. A report released by Ravi Zacharias International Ministries admitted that "we allowed our misplaced trust in Ravi to result in him having less oversight and accountability than would have been wise and loving."[11]

This type of abuse plays out on smaller scales in Christian communities all over the world. Consider Hannah's story. After successfully reporting her first experience of harassment, she worried that additional reports could make her look like a rape-baiter, so she chose to stay quiet instead. You might also remember Lily's story from chapter 5, where a man used his position as a small-group leader to pressure Lily into a romantic relationship. Lily told me that she reported his behavior to leaders at her church, but nothing happened.

Certainly, the Council on Biblical Manhood and Woman-hood doesn't condone abuse. Piper and other complementarian leaders would say that male sexual harassment is a corruption of biblical masculinity. Nevertheless, at some point, Christians must deal with the fact that reducing gender to a power relationship fosters an atmosphere in which abuse can easily flourish. It may not be the intent, but it's often the result.

The Man Haters

In 1992, Pat Robertson famously wrote, "The feminist agenda is not about equal rights for women: It is about a socialist, anti-family political movement that encourages women to leave their husbands, kill their children, practice witchcraft, destroy capitalism, and become lesbians."[12] In the opinion of many, lesbianism is the end result of the godless "feminist threat," where "feminism" doesn't actually refer to feminism but rather to the abandonment of men and the destruction of society.

In a fallen context where the defining difference between masculinity and femininity is that women look *up* to men, women who *don't need* men strain at the limits of an impoverished anthropology. Queer women find themselves afloat in Christianity with no discernible destination, flotsam and jetsam to the waters of a culture they confound. Single women share the same burden, especially as they move into their 30s with no man to supposedly "anchor" their existence. The stereotypical, heavy-footed, man-hating "dyke" thereby surfaces to channel fears, manifesting all the anxieties of a culture where women should stay in their place. As long as a woman can say, "I'm not like *that*," then maybe she can still fit in.

Here, the word *that* refers to a dominant woman. Someone who goes just an *inch* too far. Laughs just a bit too loudly. Talks just a bit too much. In other words, acts just a bit too "manly." In that sense, being "manly" doesn't have anything to do with objective notions about masculinity at all. Instead, it refers to what people see as existing beyond a woman's reach. Something above her station. The specter of lesbianism emerges to caricature this gendered offense—the burly looking, unattractive "dyke" that no man wants and that no woman should desire to be.

Consider Meredith's experience. Asserting her dignity as a queer Black woman of equal status to her white husband was enough to turn heads. She was a business professional, a strong decision-maker with an aggressive personality who often picked up her husband's tab at restaurants. She fixed things around the house while her husband cooked dinner. Meredith and her husband had a wonderful relationship, were financially stable, and were happy together. But Meredith felt like a failure, like something about her was "wrong."

In the context of a culture that attaches power dynamics to gender expression, people like Meredith become "angry Black women" who stomp all over men unless they learn to submit to male authority. In this way, being a good enough "lady" not only has to do with giving proper deference to men; it's also inextricably caught up in a culture that cannot fathom godly femininity outside of white, Anglo-Saxon norms.[13]

BURDEN 5 SUMMARY

We thus conclude the fifth burden that LGBTQ people bear in the church. "Real" men take charge, "good" ladies listen, and LGBTQ people fail to measure up.

BURDEN 6

MADE IN
THE IMAGE
OF ~~GOD~~ SEX

II. Gender Essentialism

LESLI

For Lesli, growing up in the context of the Southern Baptist Church, anything related to LGBTQ issues was a sin. "It was just viewed as this unforgiveable thing," Lesli recalled. "There was no grace for it. There was no way around it. The action was a sin. The attraction was a sin. The temptation was a sin. Even studying it would have been a sin if it was for any other purpose than proving these people are degenerate. There was no ability to study for understanding."

As a gay and nonbinary person—meaning that Lesli doesn't identify as male or female and uses they/them pronouns—Lesli wrestled with their gender and sexuality. Their pastor preached about transgender people, and Lesli, who was still closeted, realized the sermon was about them.

Lesli got up the courage to ask their pastor for help. "I think I might be like those people," Lesli said. "But I don't want to be. What do I do?"

In response, the pastor escorted Lesli out of the building and told them to never come back. "I ended up looking to the LGBTQ community for family," they recalled.

Lesli did not attend church for nearly two decades, but circumstances eventually brought them back to a different church in search of spiritual support. The pastor didn't kick them out, which was enough to give Lesli hope. When Lesli entered counseling for same-sex attraction, however, they found themself burdened by impossible expectations.

"When you have an attraction and your pupils dilate, that dilation is a sin," they recalled. "If your heart starts beating, if your palm starts sweating, that's something you need to repent." Anything that could be remotely construed as attraction was an occasion for repentance.

A trans woman named Chelsea started attending Lesli's church, but the pastor refused to use female pronouns for Chelsea and called her by her dead name, or the name that is on her birth certificate. When Lesli ventured to talk about trans issues with close friends, the friends told Lesli that Lesli was delusional and buying into the lies of Satan.

"They said that being nonbinary was just a trend," Lesli recalled. "They wouldn't even take the time to listen to why I was nonbinary. When I hear the words 'she/her,' it makes me want to cut. It makes me suicidal, . . . but my friends at church wouldn't take the time to listen."

Lesli started attending a different church but kept in touch with their old pastor. They met for coffee one day, and he mentioned Chelsea.

"I saw Nathan not too long ago," the pastor said, referring to Chelsea by her dead name. The pastor said that Chelsea had been dressed like a man and had thanked the pastor for setting her straight. The pastor sounded satisfied, so Lesli responded that it was great to hear that Chelsea was doing well.

Then the pastor mentioned that Chelsea died by suicide a few months after running into him.

Shocked, Lesli didn't know what to say. Didn't the pastor see a connection between Chelsea's suicide and pressuring her to identify as a man? Lesli cautiously pressed him for answers, but in his mind, he had done Chelsea a favor—saved her soul before she died.

"People have zero perception of anything outside of their own experience," Lesli recalled. "Dots that are so easy for anyone that has ever been marginalized to connect, for a white cis-het male with a PhD and a great job living in a beautiful house on the East Coast, those dots aren't even on the same page, much less part of the same picture."

The pastor congratulated himself on a job well done in the ministry. But Chelsea was dead.

■ ■ ■

What does it mean to be male, and what does it mean to be female? And what do you do if neither male nor female describe who you are? These questions evoke discomfort, even anger. Fights over bathroom access and women's safety merge into bigger questions about human identity and the meaning of embodiment and personhood.

For many Christians, gender essentialism provides the easiest and quickest solution. Gender essentialism teaches that certain fixed, universal traits determine identity. A person's biological sex—typically determined by their genitalia or chromosomes—determines a person's gender, which, likewise, determines a fixed male or female "nature" characterized by universal traits (e.g., women are nurturers; men are protectors).

Many Christians assume that gender essentialism ought to be obvious. As a result, adherence to gender essentialism often becomes a requirement for salvation or, at the very least, Christian maturity. It's not uncommon for Christians to invoke essentialism in conversations about trans and intersex people. Many even believe that rejecting essentialism amounts to an attack on the Christian faith.

Notably, many Christians focus almost exclusively on trans people when it comes to debates about gender identity, raising questions like, "Are you telling me it's okay for biological men to compete athletically against women?" Often these questions stem from a desire to silence and invalidate trans people. However, many do genuinely desire to learn and understand. Most readers of this book, for example, likely *do* want to learn. For you, these questions *do* come from a desire to grow.

Nevertheless, I'm going to ask you to set aside most of the questions you have about trans people and, instead, consider questions about the dominant gender narrative in many churches today. Self-reflection is the first step to growth. It's easy to question our perception of belief systems and people "out there." It's not so easy to turn that critical lens on ourselves and question the assumptions that drive our own beliefs.

How, for example, did essentialism come to be the dominant approach to gender identity in the West and, by proxy, Western Christianity? Is it really a central tenet of the Christian faith? Is it really biblical? Or is gender a much more complicated and mysterious reality than what essentialism can explain?

Questioning our own assumptions, prejudices, and biases needs to come before we ever demand answers from other people. This is uncomfortable because it puts our own allegiances under the microscope. It's a natural human tendency to deflect attention from one's own position. The result is that marginalized cultures get scrutinized to pieces even as dominant cultures go unexamined.

As we dive deeper into conversations about gender in this chapter, keep in mind that we're putting in check this fallen human tendency to scrutinize people "out there." Instead, we're embracing the discomfort of examining dominant narratives in Christian culture. In the process, you might find yourself challenged. But let's embrace that process together for the sake of a healthier church.

The Origins of Gender Essentialism

Sex and *gender* mean different things. In common parlance, sex refers to "what's between your legs," whereas gender refers to "what's between your ears"—that is, sex is an external reality, such as genitalia or chromosomes, whereas gender is an internal reality, such as personality and disposition. This means that sex refers to the *what* of human biology, and gender refers to the *who* of human identity. In this book, when I refer to trans people, I'm referring to anyone who doesn't identify with the gender assigned to them at birth. When I refer to cisgender people, I'm referring to anyone who identifies with the gender assigned to them at birth. When I refer to intersex people, I'm referring to anyone born with ambiguous sexual biology, such as people who have male chromosomes and female genitalia. Some intersex people are trans and vice versa, but the two experiences are distinct.

Gender essentialism posits that sex and gender are linked in such a way that biology determines identity—that is, sex determines gender. The earliest articulations of gender essentialism originate in Greek philosophy. Plato believed that all things could be described by their "essence." The "essence" of a thing was its universal archetype, a form that captures its "typical" state or nature.[1] Human nature, he reasoned, actually has two natures: the superior form being man and the inferior being woman.[2] Aristotle expanded on such thinking in *Generation of Animals*, in which he developed a rationale for the superiority of the male sex. Beginning in the womb, all embryos commence their development as male. Defects and deviations sometimes lead to what he called "monstrosities," referring to people born with disabilities.[3] "The first beginning of this deviation," he said, "is when a female is formed instead of a male."[4] This happens whenever the "faculty" of anatomy associated with sex fails to develop properly, resulting in the opposite of what it should have been. Female anatomy is thus an "inversion" of male anatomy. Male genitalia protrude outward and female genitalia sink inward.[5]

Aristotle's explanation of female anatomical development as "defective" provided a basis for women's inferiority. Just as the vagina is the defective opposite of a penis, so too is female emotionality the opposite of male rationality, female weakness the opposite of male strength: "As between the sexes, the male is by nature superior and the female inferior, the male ruler and the female subject."[6] As Rachel Green Miller summarizes, "According to these beliefs, women and men are completely different and have few overlapping qualities. The male body is perfect and ideal. The female body is mutilated and inverted. Men are rational; women irrational. Men are strong and courageous; women weaker and nervous. Men were made to rule; women to obey."[7]

This understanding of sex laid a foundation for the gender hierarchy in ancient Rome. The penis was powerful and made to dominate, the vagina passive and made for domination.[8] Men were equipped with a rational mind that empowered them to dominate well. Women with a uterus that floated about their bodies, inclining them to emotional outbursts.[9] The word *hysteria* descends from the Greek word for uterus, *hysterika*, as a result. In other words, male and female "parts" functioned to express the entire course of a person's existence, their place in society, and their very nature.

Inevitably, the Roman Empire disseminated such thinking across the cultures it conquered. Western civilization thus inherited from Greco-Roman society a "symbolic link"[10] between sex and gender wherein one determines the other. Assumptions about the female *sex* functioned to define the female *gender* as domestic, irrational, hysterical, and passive. Assumptions about the male *sex* functioned to define the male *gender* as political, rational, self-controlled, and powerful.[11]

The Christian Counternarrative

In chapter 7, we caught an early glimpse of Christianity's impact on Greco-Roman culture when Paul declared both husband and wife to have *equal* authority over each other's bodies (1 Cor. 7:4). Central to this idea was the Christian conception of marriage as a "one flesh" union (Matt. 19:1–12; Mark 10:2–12; Eph. 5:25–33). Such a concept would have been absurd to a Roman citizen. The female body was defective, a result of "deviations" in the womb that perverted the creation of the perfect, male body. There was no such thing as a "one flesh" union. A husband could no more share the same body with his wife than he could share the same body with a dog.

Christianity upended this logic. Husband and wife are *one* body, Christians said. *One* union of *one* flesh with *equal* authority over that flesh. No longer could a husband sleep around with whatever women (and men) he desired, nor could he divorce his wife whenever he saw fit. No longer could he relate to his wife as dominator over dominated. *His* body was his *wife's* body, and his wife *owned* his body the *same way* that he did hers.

Now he had to love her just as he loved his own body.

"He who loves his wife loves himself," Paul said. "For no one ever hated his own flesh, but nourishes and cherishes it, just as Christ does the church, because we are members of his body" (Eph. 5:28–30). Not only were husband and wife one and the same flesh, but they were also equal members of the *one* body of Jesus Christ and fellow heirs to the kingdom. Consider Paul's exhortation to the church in Galatia: "But now that faith has come, we are no longer under a guardian, for in Christ Jesus you are all sons of God, through faith. For as many of you as were baptized into Christ have put on Christ. There is neither Jew nor Greek, there is neither slave nor free, there is no male and female, for you are all one in Christ Jesus. And if you are Christ's, then you are Abraham's offspring, heirs according to promise" (Gal. 3:25–29).

There is no "male and female," Paul says. "You are *all sons* of God." To modern readers, this might sound offensive, erasing "daughters" from the picture. But consider it in the context of Paul's day. In a culture where only *men* could be citizens and only *sons* could inherit the father's wealth and only *males* were considered fully human, Paul declared both male *and* female to be equal heirs to the kingdom of heaven. "For you are all *one* in Christ Jesus," he said, "heirs according to promise." Women were humans of equal dignity. They were *sons*. In effect, they were "men."

This sounds radical even today. Decades of culture-war rhetoric have trained us to bristle at the idea of someone's daughter being their "son." We're taught to see such things as an attack on the Christian faith and created order. And yet we find this type of language in the Bible itself. Christianity declared the body of the husband and the body of the wife to be one and the same body united by one and the same Savior, meaning that *all* could be sons of God and heirs to the kingdom of heaven. This language sounds radical because it is.

It's no surprise that Christianity attracted women from the start. Women were the first to witness the resurrection and the first to declare that Christ was risen (Luke 24:1–12). Paul described women repeatedly as co-laborers in the church (Rom. 16:1, 3, 6, 7, 15; 1 Cor. 16:19; Phil. 4:2–3; Col. 4:15), and Mary Magdalene is revered throughout Christian history as the "apostle to the apostles" (John 20:11–18). Women even openly prayed and prophesied in the context of church assemblies (1 Cor. 11:5).

Modern readers get confused by passages like 1 Corinthians 11 that required women to adorn head coverings. But again, in a cultural context where head coverings symbolized the authority of a husband, enforcing a system where *every* woman adorned a head covering, regardless of marital status, dismantled the need for women to marry to gain respectability. Women with husbands *and* women without husbands enjoyed *equal* standing in the assembly of God. Even prostitutes could wear the veil. Sarah Ruden explains the significance:

> All Christian women were to cover their heads in church, without distinction of beauty, wealth, respectability—or of privilege so great as to allow toying with traditional appearances. . . . If the women complied—and later church tradition suggests they did—you could have looked at a congregation and not necessarily been able to tell who was an honored wife and mother and who had been forced, or maybe was still being forced, to

service twenty or thirty men a day. This had never happened in any public gathering before.[12]

The idea that women didn't need a husband to validate their existence rocked the foundations of the Roman social order. The fact that Paul encouraged celibacy only made things worse. Young women started refusing to get married! Stories spread of Christian women seducing their husbands into *celibacy*. According to Ruden, mythologies even developed about Christian female prostitutes turning their would-be male clients into rock.[13]

To be clear, Paul wasn't trying to say that the male sex and the female sex don't exist or don't matter; it would be quite a stretch to say that Paul was attempting to abolish gender. Rather, Christianity took aim at the Greco-Roman conception of sex and gender that disenfranchised women by robbing them of their full humanity, a conception justified by philosophical pontifications about human biological development, the perfection of the male body, and the deficiency of the female body. New Testament writers might not have been saying that sex and gender don't matter, but they were certainly dismantling the ways that sex and gender mattered in the pagan context of ancient Rome.

12. More Than Just Monkeys?

JACK

Jack had always been a "sissy boy" growing up, opting to be the princess in video games, crying often and sometimes donning dresses and pretty hats and jewelry.

But God was masculine, Jack was taught, and he internalized the belief that "maleness and masculinity were inherently more like God than femaleness and femininity."

"I had a lot of shame about being different in ways that I was taught made me unacceptable," said Jack, whose pronouns are he/they, "like I was not worthy of love in the same way that other people were. . . . If you had one set of genitalia, then you should look like Ward Cleaver, and if you had another set of genitalia, you should look like June Cleaver."

The school where Jack attended invited a guest speaker who said simply and clearly, "You can't be gay and Christian." Jack didn't know what to make of it, especially as they found themself feeling things for boys and girls. "Christians taught us at church and school that being gay was about the worst thing you could be. God's grace covered any sin except that."

Jack stuffed their feelings down and tried to lean into "being a man." However, when Jack started dating a woman, they couldn't understand why *she* was the one pressuring *Jack* to have sex. Jack was attracted to her. So why wasn't Jack tempted to have sex all the time? Wasn't that how men were supposed to be "wired"?

When Jack married the same girlfriend, they felt ashamed about their sex drive, as though it made them less of a man. "I thought I was supposed to want sex multiple times a day. But a lot of times I just wanted takeout." Eventually, Jack and their wife started biblical counseling, which focused almost exclusively on Jack's bisexuality and gender fluidity. "It was all trying to get me to look like the 'right' type of man." No fingernail polish. No pink. No wearing soft textures. It all became a maze of rules and regulations.

"A lot of it stemmed from this belief that the Bible unambiguously teaches that men should be leaders, combined with a fetishization of power," Jack recalled. "It left me decidedly on the outside of what humanity was supposed to look like."

Everything reached a breaking point when the ministerial leadership convinced Jack's wife to get an exorcist. Jack underwent several exorcisms but came out of it queer every time. The church eventually excommunicated Jack and his wife.

"The constant messaging was that gender and sexuality are supposed to look a certain way, but it didn't look like that for me," Jack said. "It made me feel like I deserved to be treated as subhuman."

Jack's life revolved around being the perfect man. But then one day, Jack suffered a major stroke, leaving them disabled—paralyzed in one arm and walking with a limp. Biblical manhood felt further away than ever. How could he ever be the right kind of man when everything about him was "wrong"?

"My increasingly desperate attempts to remain in non-affirming churches were part of an effort to prove to myself and to other people that I could be the right kind of gay," Jack said. "Any mistreatment that I received I thought I deserved it, or that it was worth it in the long run. . . . I believed that if I were the right kind of gay that I'd become worthy of love."[1]

LIANNE

Lianne was born with an intersex condition called mixed gonadal dysgenesis. Some of her cells had a Y chromosome, but others didn't. As a result, she had a mix of ovarian and testicular tissue, couldn't have vaginal intercourse, and had a number of medical issues.

Doctors wrote male on her birth certificate and sent her home. Her parents raised Lianne as a boy, but she knew that she wasn't their son.

In high school, a pastor shared the Romans road with her, and she prayed the sinner's prayer. "I assumed that my bodily differences were my fault, so maybe if I prayed hard enough, God would make me a real boy." Instead, "It became more and more difficult to pretend to be someone different on the outside than I was on the inside."

In college, guys on campus made fun of her. At one point, someone scratched the words "Little Queen" on her door. Others called her "Clit." One of her roommates would pin her to the wall and threaten to rape her. It was a regular cycle of humiliation wherever she went. One day, security caught her sunbathing in a dress. They demanded to see her ID, which didn't match her physical appearance. The dean summoned her and threatened to expel her if she didn't see one of the school's therapists. So she cut her hair short, bought a motorcycle, and went to her appointments.

But getting a haircut accomplished little, so she sought the opinion of a doctor. He told her that people would accept her as a woman. Tired of her life revolving around her inability to function socially as a man or sexually as a male, she decided to change her legal status to female. Suddenly, people welcomed her.

After that, Lianne kept her experience as an intersex woman private, at least at church. However, a friend eventually stumbled on something she'd written online and told one of the church elders. After a meeting that lasted several hours, the pastor instructed her to reject "anything LGBTQ related." Later, some in her denomination started talking about how sex is immutable and eternal. One person even told her that *angels* have a sex because the Bible calls them "he."

146

It baffled Lianne.

"The male-female binary is so important to some Christians that they read these ideas back into Scripture," she said. "Article 7 of the Nashville Statement says that my gender has to be based on the sex I would have been in the garden of Eden. There's no allowance for the body God knit together in my mother's womb. To them, the Y chromosome I have in some of my cells is the final indication of God's intent for my life. But no matter what the doctors do to my body, I'll still be intersex. Saying I'm male doesn't make it so. All I can do is try to glorify God with the body I have."

■ ■ ■

Greco-Roman essentialism grew up under the auspices of a conquering empire that believed its people superior to the "barbarian" tribes. This provided justification for the conquest of "lesser" races under the guise of spreading civilization. Not only was the Roman male body superior to the female body; it was superior to disabled bodies, "barbarian" bodies, and basically every other people under the sun. When the Italian Renaissance sparked a revival in Greco-Roman culture in the fourteenth century, such thinking was tailor-made for the colonial impulses that gripped much of Europe following the discovery of a "new world."

Faulty assumptions about human biology became more important than ever in the new colonial order. Comparisons of skin color and brain size offered supposed proof of white supremacy. "Savages" were the new barbarians, and twisted rationality became "scientific." "Biological determinism here intersects with scientific racism," observes sociologist Amy Ansell, "in providing justification for slavery and colonialism, and later, disenfranchisement and segregation."[2]

No aspect of human nature was left untouched, including gender. Darwin reasoned that natural selection impacted the male sex more rigorously than the female, causing the male species to be more highly evolved. Males had to defend their females and young, fight off enemies, hunt for sustenance, and fashion weapons, tailoring their biology to be the stronger and fitter of the sexes. Herbert Spencer, who was a contemporary of Darwin, argued that the existence of sex inequality was biologically determined.[3]

Such thinking fueled resistance to women's suffrage in the early 1900s and reached a near fever pitch following the second wave of the feminist movement in the 1960s.[4] In one article among many of its kind, anthropologist Lionel Tiger argued that the exclusion of women from seats of power had "biological origins." Males and females, he said, have "genetically programmed behavioural propensities" that make men suited for political, economic, military, and other "power-dominance-centered subsystems" and women better suited for domestic fields.[5]

Biologist Edward O. Wilson then extrapolated from his studies of insect biology and built an entire theory of human social life. According to Wilson, the sexual dance between male and female, sperm and egg, aggressor and aggressed, plays a pivotal role in human evolution. This dance provides a "mechanism" through which certain genetic realities evolved to make the male and female sex what they are today.[6]

Wilson's theories spawned the entire subfield of sociobiology, a field in which Darwin's outdated ideas about sexual evolution were dusted off and reused with new science to back them up: Men were "natural" aggressors suited for power and dominance because of their highly evolved sexual functions. Women were natural nurturers because their sexual functions evolved in response to men's. Some went so far as to offer male biology as an explanation for rape and violence.[7]

The *Imago Dei*

It's no surprise that contemporary examples of misogyny, racism, xenophobia, and ableism, among many other issues, commonly allude to essentialism. Social Darwinists believed that everything from criminal activity to intelligence to laziness could be traced to the evolution of certain biological traits, fueling the notion that we can manipulate society through natural selection. If biology determines identity, then we can determine the direction of the human race by controlling its biology. Such thinking can be traced to some of the worst atrocities in modern times, including not only the trans-Atlantic slave trade but also the horrors of the Holocaust in World War II and modern eugenics.

The frustrating thing for many scientists is that essentialism often holds true in the animal kingdom. Wilson's sociobiological determinism *can* be demonstrated in the context of things like ant colonies (his specialty). However, despite decades of effort to the contrary, no proof yet exists for a causative link between biology and social identity in humans. If you pay attention to studies that purport to explain male and female identity through biology, *animals* are always the subject of study. Human studies rebuff these theories.

The question is why? Why do humans confound essentialism? From an evolutionary perspective, humans are part of the animal kingdom. If it works for animals, why wouldn't it work for humans?

In the context of my own upbringing, Christians have always had an answer: *We are not monkeys,* I learned. *Human beings are more than just a bunch of mutations under a microscope.*[8] Humans are made in the image of God. As bearers of the *imago Dei*, we carry within our very nature the truth about the Almighty himself. At the core of human identity is something infinitely mysterious and unsearchable.

Is the science behind genetics and biological development useful? Absolutely. Does it lead to helpful discoveries in the realm of medicine and public health? Unquestionably. But will it ever be able to tell us the *who* of human identity? Certainly not.

Biology does not and *cannot* tell us who we are. As helpful as it might be to understand a person's genetic history, especially in the realm of medicine, it can't tell us who that person is. Human nature can't be broken down into a list of predictive traits. Human beings are more than just monkeys.

Deep down, we know that essentialism is dehumanizing. If someone tries to apply it to us, we get angry. "Who are you to tell me that I can't be good at math just because I'm a woman?" "You think I can't be educated just because I'm Black?" "Just because I'm poor doesn't make me lazy."

This is the reason that essentialism often gets used by one group of people to explain the existence of *another* group of people in a way that invalidates their existence. During the women's suffrage movement men tried to keep women from gaining the vote by attempting to prove their biological inferiority. In response, feminists fought fiercely against essentialism for *themselves* but often reinforced it for people of color, lobbying for white women's right to vote but not for Black women's. Gay people, as another example, fought hard against essentialism during the gay rights movement, pushing back against the narrative of perversion. However, many fall back on essentialism when it comes to trans people, remaining apathetic about—or even opposed to—trans rights.

Gender Essentialism in Christianity

In summer 2020, I had an interesting series of interactions on Twitter. A pastor shared a quote from Matt Moore, a celibate, same-sex-attracted man. The quote came from an article published in 2016 by the Gospel Coalition. In the article, now retracted, Moore said, "I could be straight as an arrow but still fall terribly short of manhood if I didn't submit my heterosexuality to the revealed will of God. It's more masculine to be mainly attracted to men yet obedient to God than it is to be mainly attracted to women and disobedient to God. A celibate same-sex-attracted guy is far more of a man than a womanizing guy who bows to the will of his sex drive."[9]

Here, Moore expressed a view of masculinity rooted in obedience to God, not sexuality. Biblical masculinity doesn't depend on sexual attraction to the opposite sex. It doesn't depend on sex at all. It depends on our obedience to God.

However, many reacted harshly.

Reformed theologian James White commented, "Is it not rather obvious that 'masculine' as an adjective requires a definition of the noun from which it is derived, and that, biblically, there is no positive foundation for defining manhood in light of the universal condemnation of SSA [same-sex attraction] in holy Writ?" Pastor Tom Buck said, "God created masculinity and there's NOTHING 'masculine' about a man being attracted to another man." He then clarified in later comments, "God created men by design. . . . What it MEANS to be a man sexually . . . is attraction to women."

As I engaged with Buck, I found his initial argument to be the following: Attraction to women, by definition, is a masculine trait and an *essential* component to masculine identity. Therefore, a man *cannot* be masculine if he is attracted to men. A man can *only* be masculine if he is attracted to women. The implication is that a man's identity is defined by his sexuality.[10]

How is it that a Christian pastor could believe that men are masculine *only* if they're attracted to women? On its face, it's nonsensical. But if you follow the line we've traced from the beginning of the book until now, it's consistent.

Many Christians can't fathom a biblically "masculine" man who is same-sex attracted because, in their minds, being a man means having a sexual biology that responds to the female sex in sexual ways. John Piper, for example, quotes the late theologian Paul Jewett favorably when he says, "Sexuality permeates one's individual being to its very depth; it conditions every facet of one's life as a person. . . . Our self-knowledge is indissolubly bound up not simply with our human being but with our sexual being. At the human level there is no 'I and thou' per se, but only the 'I' who is male or female confronting the 'thou,' the 'other' who is also male or female."[11]

Consider the implications of this quote, which can be found in *Recovering Biblical Manhood and Womanhood*. Many Christians accuse LGBTQ people of defining themselves by sex, and yet here, we find Christians doing the very thing many claim that LGBTQ people do. Here, in the classic Christian text on biblical manhood and womanhood, we find human identity defined as "indissolubly bound up" in our "sexual being." There is no "I." There is only "male or female" responding to another "male or female" in heterosexual ways. For all the finger-pointing at LGBTQ people for supposedly making sex the sum total of their identity, the predominant evangelical approach to gender identity defines human beings by sex.

The Consequences

In the context of sexual ethics and gender identity, trans and intersex people experience the worst consequences. They learn that one or two facts about their biology or genetic code ought to determine everything about who they are. A trans woman can't possibly be a woman because she was born with a penis. A trans man can't possibly be a man because he was born with a vagina. An intersex woman can't possibly be a woman, *even though* she has a vagina, because her genetic chromosomes are XY, not XX.

Heath Lambert, formerly the executive director of the Association of Certified Biblical Counselors, says that parents should teach their children that boys and girls who struggle with their gender identity are *sinning*. "That little boy on the news is fighting God's Word just the way you do when you behave cruelly toward your sister." Children who question their gender identity are a "parental problem" needing "discipline," he explains.[12]

New Testament theologian Robert Gagnon says that trans people rebel against the "structures of maleness or femaleness created by God." These structures are "chromosomes, genitalia and numerous other external features, hormones, and at least some dimorphic brain structures." He concludes, "Scripture regards such attempts at overriding one's birth-sex as abhorrent."[13]

Certainly, things like chromosomes and genitalia and other biological features are important. Someone born with a penis will undoubtedly have different experiences than someone born with a vagina. Likewise for someone with XX chromosomes instead of XY, as well as for someone with more testosterone than estrogen. But are *these* differences the defining differences between men and women?

Gagnon's logic rests on the belief that "complementarity of the sexes" defines marriage and therefore gender. However, the way such logic breaks down is troublesome. It amounts to the following: Gender identity is complementary in the same way that biological sex is complementary. We know that biological sex is complementary because a penis fits perfectly into a vagina to make children. Therefore, men are men and women are women. Gagnon might not put it this way, but this is what you get in laymen's terms. You effectively reduce human identity to penises complementing vaginas.

At the end of the day, it's hard to see how such logic is any different than Aristotle's explanation of women's inferiority because a vagina is the inversion of a penis. Gagnon's observations about differences in biological sex function to validate his prior belief that men and women ought to complement each other in the roles they adopt in marriage, family, and society. While it might be possible to make a theological case for sexual ethics based on the procreative capacity of the male and female sex (Lesli, for example, is celibate due to their convictions in this regard), it's a bit of a stretch to infer an entire explanation for human *identity* based on the differences between a penis and a vagina. We effectively reduce gender to a collection of reproductive organs.

Recovering Biblical Manhood and Womanhood relies heavily on animal studies in its discussion of "biological predeterminants."[14] Such reliance exposes an uncomfortable reality. Essentialist thinkers rely on animal studies to cushion the existing research. The Council on Biblical Manhood and Womanhood frames the "root" biological differences between men and women as "characteristic not only of humans but of many of the higher social animals."[15]

But reducing human nature to biological facts, the way a scientist might study the animal kingdom, is always—predictably—dehumanizing. The end trajectory of such approaches turns men into sex-crazed animals and women into their sexual objects. Should men ever "stumble," it's not their fault. It's just their biology.

Growing up in the broader culture of evangelicalism, I learned through various teachers that a man is "biologically wired" to respond to my body sexually and that I am therefore just as responsible for his lust. I sat through multiple sermons as a teen where women who "cause men to stumble" were discussed in light of the Matthew 18:6 injunction, where Jesus says, "Whoever causes one of these little ones who believe in me to sin, it would be better for him to have a great millstone fastened around his neck and to be drowned in the depth of the sea." As an adult, I attended a church for a number of years where I couldn't have a conversation alone with the male pastor.

Thoughtful Christians express dismay at the hypersexualization of relationships between men and women. But hypersexualization is what you get when you cultivate a theology that reduces the relationship between sex and gender to biology. Powerful voices in the church start saying things like "males are more visually spring-loaded to lust" and females are "wired to want men to notice their bodies."[16] Men may be responsible for the sins they commit toward women, but women are just as responsible for the sins they commit in *causing* men to sin. In the words of Kevin DeYoung, "Some people want to see pornography and others want to be pornography."[17]

The pornographic definition of gender originates in essentialist thinking, and societies that adopt essentialism inevitably devolve into hypersexuality. A system that caters almost exclusively to the perceived sexual needs of cisgender men leaves a trail of rape, abuse, and assault in its wake. Many Christians shake their heads in bewilderment at the number of male Christian leaders falling to sexual assault allegations by the day, but this phenomenon is a telltale sign of the hypersexuality that is endemic to essentialism.

I'm reminded of Jack's experience. Jack described feeling ashamed of themself for wanting to have sex less frequently than their wife. Jack felt it made them "less" of a man. In Jack's circles, an unspoken understanding existed that sex and power are inextricably connected to manhood. Men are "wired" to want sex; women are "wired" to give it to them; and within this sexual "wiring," we can somehow find the definition of gender. It left Jack feeling that God had somehow "wired" them wrong.

Embracing the Mysterious

At the end of the day, saying that a man isn't a "real" man unless he is heterosexual and saying that a man isn't a "real" man unless he has a penis are only different as a matter of degree. Dominos in the same line. The implications are far-reaching, and troubling questions arise.

Who is better positioned to know the *who* of someone's identity? A pastor who can theologize about your sexual attraction? A doctor who can tell you if it's a penis or a vagina? A scientist with a microscope who can isolate your chromosomes? Computers in a lab? If so, how does that square with a view of human nature that says human beings are more than just monkeys? We check the genitals of animals to know what they are. But human beings are made in the image of God. We talk to human beings to learn *who* they are.

So what exactly do Christians suggest about trans and intersex people when they demand to know about their genitalia and genetics and hormones? Do Christians really understand the *imago Dei*? Or do Christians reduce God's image to biology and genetics and nothing more?

These questions might be startling. They might even feel threatening. But as Christians, it's imperative that we sit in that place of discomfort. It's the same place of discomfort that our trans and intersex siblings experience every day. This doesn't mean that sexual biology is unimportant. Nor does it mean that many cisgender people don't experience their sexual biology as a central component to their identity. Nor does it mean that trans and intersex people don't experience their *own* sexual biology in ways that are varied and important. But it does mean that Christians need to consider the ways they diminish the *imago Dei* by attempting to universalize the cisgender, heterosexual experience of sexual biology.

As an intersex woman, Lianne was told that she must identify as a man for no other reason than because she has a Y chromosome. Certainly, God created the male and female sex in the garden of Eden. But it's a stretch to take this fact and claim that sexual biology ought to determine the identity of every single person ever created in the image of God. As Lianne pointed out to me, this requires "reading back" gender essentialism into the biblical narrative. Intersex people like Lianne, who don't neatly fit the sexual categories in the garden of Eden, expose the limitations of sexual reductionism. God made Adam and Eve male and female, but God also made Lianne, a woman who is both. Her experience of womanhood is not a "sign of the fall." Her womanhood is made in the image of God like anyone else's.

Some Christians, however, hear stories of intersex people like Lianne, and instead of recognizing that something might be insufficient about essentialism, they only buckle down. The existence of intersex people, they say, proves that trans people have no biological reason to question their gender identity. Such arguments display an attachment to essentialism that challenges the bounds of rationality. Certainly, biology is important, but if we treat biology as the be-all and end-all of human nature, we erase the complexity of human existence.

Human beings are biological creatures, but if there's anything to be learned from the trans and intersex experience, it's that not all human beings experience their biology in the same way. We don't yet actually *know* what the relationship between sex and gender entails, and that should give us humility. Science can't yet explain everything, and it probably never will. Christians, of all people, should expect this. Transgender writer Austen Hartke puts it well:

> We don't know why people are transgender. That is, we don't yet know the scientific or medical reason behind the fact that a percentage of humans on earth—1.4 million adults in the United States alone—have a gender identity that doesn't match the sex they were assigned at birth. Could it be the hormones we're exposed to in the womb? Could it be caused by some rogue genetic material? Maybe it has to do with the way our brains are wired in the first two years of life, when we're learning so much so fast. Or perhaps there's some kind of learned component that has to do with the way we perceive gender as we grow. Maybe it's a combination of all of these things. The fact is that right now it's a mystery.[18]

Mysteries make people uncomfortable, but Christians of all people should know how to embrace the mysterious. The gospel itself is a mystery (Eph. 3; Col. 2:1–3), and we worship an "unsearchable" God, a God whose image we bear. As the *imago Dei*, we human beings should expect to find the mysterious and unsearchable etched into the fabric of our being. Why be quick to append simplistic answers to something so eternal?

When Christians use biological sex as the definitive marker of trans people's identity, it leads to despair. It denies trans people the right to move and breathe and live in the world as human beings who are more than just a collection of reproductive organs. When Lesli, for example, asked their friends to use "they/them" pronouns instead of "she/her," Lesli wasn't looking to cause trouble. They were looking for a way to *exist*. It was a matter of *life and death*.

Lesli is alive to tell their story today, but their trans friend Chelsea is not. Chelsea's church never gave her a chance to exist in the complexity and fullness of her humanity. They gave her sexual biology instead, and in so doing, they gave her death.

BURDEN 6 SUMMARY

We thus conclude the sixth burden that LGBTQ people bear in the church. The Bible says that human beings are made in the image of God. But many Christians ask LGBTQ people to be made in the image of their sex and sex alone.

BURDEN 7

JESUS ~~SAVES~~
DAMNS

13. Vessels of Wrath

NATALIE

Natalie knew something was different about her as early as age six. She was a girl, and yet her parents told her that she needed to be a boy. She couldn't quite articulate it, but she knew that something was wrong. By the age of twelve, Natalie's prayers became the same every night: "Dear God, if you're the God of miracles, then make one happen. Let me wake up a girl. Nobody else has to know. I know you can do it."

Natalie would conclude her prayer with one final request: "And if you're not going to give me that miracle, just kill me."

But Natalie awoke every morning, and every morning a boy looked back in the mirror. She wanted to talk to someone, but she couldn't. She'd heard the sermons at church condemning people like her to eternal conscious torment. "You don't question," Natalie recalled. "There's no dialogue."

One day, during high school at her Christian academy, the chapel leaders turned off all the lights so that it was pitch black in the room and instructed everybody to scream at the top of their lungs. Natalie screamed into the dark along with the rest of her friends, their lungs building a cacophony of shrieks and cries and howls.

When the lights turned on, everybody settled down, and the preacher said, "Okay. Now, imagine screaming like that in the worst fire you could

161

possibly imagine for all of eternity." The room grew deathly quiet. "Who wants to get saved?"

A sickened feeling settled in the pit of Natalie's stomach. "It was this deep, just all-encompassing fear," Natalie recalled. God hated her. She was destined for eternal damnation.

Natalie did the only thing she could think to do. She decided to become the most masculine of men she could possibly be. She built up a personality for herself around aggression and violence and macho power. In college, she and her friends designed T-shirts with the name of their school listed above the words, "NO FAGS ALLOWED."

One day, a gay boy in Natalie's church back home accused their minister of molestation. "It shook the church," Natalie recalled. "The minister was one of those people who was universally respected, loved among the youth group." Natalie refused to believe the minister was at fault. Instead, she blamed the gay community and threatened to go on a shooting spree at the local gay club.

"I wanted to lash out against the homosexual community—this community that I had been raised to believe was inherently evil," Natalie recalled. "I was angry at who the church always told me to be angry at, but it was also internal anger, anger at who I am."

After graduating from college, Natalie enlisted in the Army and joined the infantry, thinking the military would keep her masculine. But no matter how hard she tried, she couldn't escape a gut-level knowledge that she was a woman. She got up every morning and told herself, "I will put on that masculine show to escape the hellfire and brimstone."

But it wasn't working. In all her attempts to escape damnation, she was already living a hell on earth.

■ ■ ■

The first time I remember listening to a sermon about LGBTQ people was around the age of eleven. I'd definitely heard other sermons that had mentioned LGBTQ issues, but this sermon was the one that stuck. It was about the "vessels of wrath" prepared by God for "destruction" (Rom. 9:22). It wasn't about

LGBTQ people exclusively, but the pastor referenced LGBTQ people as an example. They were the ones whom God had given over to a "debased mind" (1:28) in order to "show his wrath and to make known his power" (9:22). This is why God struck them with AIDS—a "due penalty for their error" (1:27). They were "storing up wrath" for themselves on the last day, when God's "righteous judgment" would be revealed (2:5).

The sermon planted itself in my mind so vividly because it was my first conscious introduction to LGBTQ people—where I was actually aware that Christians were talking about a distinct group. The pastor bemoaned their "stealing the rainbow." When I asked an adult to explain what he meant, they told me that our pastor was talking about "sinful" people who "rebelled against God."

Being a highly visual person, I constructed in my mind an image of LGBTQ people that would follow me for years to come. Whenever queer people came up in conversation, the first thing I would imagine was a bunch of frolicking, phrenetic heathens in a terribly frenzy, dressed up in rainbow-colored apparel and laughing at God as they danced their way to hell.

So when I figured out that I was gay a decade later, it was a shock. Suddenly my life brimmed with a host of questions I had never been prepared to answer. Each question bore the possibility of storing up God's wrath against me if I answered it wrong. Being Reformed, I couldn't lose my salvation. So the next logical thought—to my horror—was that I had never been saved in the first place. I reached a point where I concluded that it might be my eternal destination to follow Jesus my entire life but still go to hell at the end of it.

At the time, I was navigating two competing chronic illnesses that were doing a good job of making my daily life miserable. It started making a twisted kind of sense that I was ill. People said that AIDS was a "due penalty" for homosexuality; maybe God was doing something similar to me. I started having panic attacks, sometimes daily. At one point, I lay awake in bed for an entire night, deathly afraid to close my eyes lest I open them again in the fires of hell.

Fearing an eternal damnation from which not even Jesus can save you is a psychological and spiritual terror that no words can fully describe. It cuts LGBTQ people off from the gospel and introduces them to a nightmare religion, a faith in which everything about your eternal destination hinges on sex and gender.

Natalie built for herself an entire life in which her Christian faith amounted to a daily performance of masculinity. For others, faith turns into a frantic commitment to sexual purity. It becomes a dizzying maze of desperate attempts to navigate both sexual ethics and gender identity, but the stakes are so high that it's often impossible to think clearly about anything beyond a paralyzing fear that eventually—despite your love for Jesus— you'll inevitably make a mistake and condemn yourself to hell.

When Christians teach that LGBTQ people need to get gender and sexuality "right" in order to win God's love, they predicate God's favor on works of human righteousness, substituting the gospel for a religion of moralism. God's free gift of grace becomes conditional. Many LGBTQ people feel *safer* gravitating toward toxic extremes, like male violence, instead of honestly exploring their gender and sexuality. In Natalie's case, becoming a violent man felt like a better way to assure salvation than grappling with the sense that she was a woman.

You might also remember Bryan from earlier in the book. He's the one whose Christian schoolmates tied him to a tree and beat him nearly unconscious, inscribing the word *fag* across his forehead. At church, the kids in youth group subjected him to beatings, ostensibly to "butch him up." We left Bryan homeless at the age of seventeen, kicked out by his mother who couldn't accept that her son was gay. He was preparing to kill himself with a shotgun in the back of his truck.

By the grace of God, on the same night he had chosen to die, a group of Christians invited him to a church service with pizza.

He decided to attend as a way to enjoy a final meal, thinking to himself, "At least I won't die hungry." Circumstances worked in such a way that he never killed himself.

The way stories like this go, we expect to hear that the service he attended somehow changed his life forever, causing him to recommit his life to Jesus Christ, renounce his homosexuality, and transition into the bliss of being born-again. But the real story is a lot more complicated.

Bryan *did* meet Jesus that night. It wasn't the Christians who attended the service, and it definitely wasn't the band, which he described as being "God-awful." It was Jesus.

"There was this warmth, this presence that came upon me," he described, "and all I could do was fall on my knees and say, 'You are Lord, and I am not.'"

However, Bryan's newfound love for Jesus was not enough for other Christians, who taught that being gay was abhorrent to God. Over time, he came to the conclusion that his faith in Jesus couldn't save him. Still, he soldiered on, trying to please a God who was disgusted by his existence.

"I started feeling really called to follow Jesus," Bryan said. "I was gonna pursue celibacy. I was like, 'Jesus doesn't want gay sex, so I can at least do that for him because I love him. Even if he doesn't love me, even if I am going to go to hell.'"

Eventually, he reached a breaking point. "I believed that Jesus didn't love me and that perhaps I was elected to be damned," he recalled. "I remember telling Jesus, 'I want you. I love you. I need you. But you don't want me, and I can't keep living this way.'" So Bryan left the faith, wanting Jesus desperately but convinced that Jesus didn't want him.

Returning to the Gospel

When Christians attach the possibility of hell to conversations about sexual ethics and gender identity, they negate the power of the gospel. It effectively reduces the Christian faith to whether a person believes the right thing about sex. It becomes impossible for LGBTQ people to authentically explore what the Bible actually says because what if they get it wrong? What if they're too lenient? Many decide that it's better to be safe than to play with fire, adopting the harshest and most legalistic approaches imaginable as a way to ward off damnation.

Countless LGBTQ people thereby come to pursue celibacy, opposite-sex marriage, or gender conformity[1] for no other reason than because they might go to hell if they don't. In effect, they rely on sex to save them, leading to a cycle of sin-guilt-repentance-repeat that leads inevitably to despair. Matthias Roberts describes the cycle well:

> Internalizing our shame, we work to take every thought captive. We start building elaborate rules, strategies, and methods of accountability to eradicate any sexual thought or feeling that falls outside of the proper context. Sometimes the rules, strategies, and accountability techniques work, but most often they don't. We mess up.
>
> Messing up intensifies our shame, leading us to believe that we are even worse than before. We believe we don't have enough self-control, or we're not trying hard enough, or we aren't good enough. We believe our sexual feelings and thoughts are too much. We heap new shame on top of our already existing shame.
>
> We double down on our attempts to control our feelings, establishing more rules and more strategies. This creates a vicious cycle. Shame rules.[2]

Trapped in a cycle of shame, people like Bryan conclude that being both gay and Christian is impossible, contradicting the life-giving message of Jesus Christ and producing nothing but anguish. Anguish, in turn, becomes a twisted way to confirm your faith, a supposed sign of the Holy Spirit's conviction. But this "conviction" only reassures you of God's condemnation. Your hopelessness feels complete.

A theological system that drives its adherents to despair of salvation itself is a theological system that lacks the gospel. Holy Spirit conviction doesn't produce death in the lives of God's children. It produces hope and life and "salvation without regret": "Godly grief," the Bible says, "produces a repentance that leads to salvation without regret, whereas worldly grief produces death" (2 Cor. 7:10). Losing hope in one's salvation comes not through the conviction of the Spirit but through the lies of the devil. There's no room for despair in Spirit-filled theology.

But What about Sin?

Many Christians recognize that something is deeply wrong with the above situation. Salvation is a free gift from God to all people, a result of grace through faith, "not a result of works, so that no one may boast" (Eph. 2:9). Nevertheless, many Christians wrestle with passages in Scripture that say the "sexually immoral" will "not inherit the kingdom of God" (Gal. 5:19–21; see also Rom. 1:18–32; 1 Cor. 6:9–10; Rev. 21:8). If that's the case, shouldn't it stand to reason that believing the wrong thing about sex—and acting accordingly—condemns you?

The problem is that this line of thinking stops short of the gospel message. Romans 1 begins with a no-holds-barred condemnation of every kind of immorality, yes, but doing so sets the stage for Romans 2, where Paul turns the tables to condemn the self-righteous. "Therefore you have no excuse, O man, every one of you who judges," he declares. "For in passing judgment on another you condemn yourself, because you, the judge, practice the very same things" (Rom. 2:1). The self-righteous stand in judgment over those who steal even as they are thieves themselves (v. 21). They look down on the sexually immoral even as they are adulterers (v. 22). They detest those who worship idols even as they rob temples (v. 22). They boast in the law of God even as they break the law themselves (v. 23). "The name of God is blasphemed among the Gentiles because of you," Paul quotes from the Prophets (v. 24).

Paul thus lays the groundwork to introduce the gospel message. The root issue is not that some people follow God's law and some people don't. It's that "none is righteous, no, not one" (Rom. 3:10). Even the most ostentatious works of righteousness cannot save. Indeed, it's for this reason that Jesus's primary condemnation against the religious leaders in Mark 7 focuses not on their outward righteousness but on their hearts: "This people honors me with their lips," he says, "but their heart is far from me" (v. 6). Outward acts can't make a sinful heart righteous any more than a righteous heart sinful. "There is nothing outside a person that by going into him can defile him," Jesus says (v. 15). What defiles a person comes "out of the heart of man" (v. 21). This is why the work of Christ entails a change of heart—a spiritual circumcision that secures a person's belonging to God. Salvation doesn't start with external change. It starts with internal regeneration.

"For no one is a Jew who is merely one outwardly, nor is circumcision outward and physical," Paul explains. "But a Jew is one inwardly, and circumcision is a matter of the heart, by the Spirit, not by the letter" (Rom. 2:28–29). This idea, that circumcision is a matter of the heart, speaks profoundly to a person's belonging within the family of God. God's covenant with his chosen people is no longer a covenant of the flesh but of the Spirit. We are God's people not because of who we are on the outside but because of the Spirit at work *inside* of us. As Jeremiah prophesied, "Behold, the days are coming, declares the LORD, when I will make a new covenant with the house of Israel. . . . I will put my law within them, and I will write it on their hearts" (31:31, 33).

Of course, people don't get to sin willy-nilly because of the Spirit's work. To borrow the words of Paul, "Are we to continue in sin that grace may abound? By no means!" (Rom. 6:1–2). The security that we enjoy in the family of God is never a license to sin. It is a license to follow our Savior. "You who were once slaves of sin," Paul says, "have become obedient from the heart . . . and, having been set free from sin, have become slaves of righteousness" (vv. 17–18). Does that mean we're suddenly perfect? Of course not. Our newfound role as "slaves to righteousness" is a slavery "leading to sanctification" (v. 19). "Now that you have been set free from sin and have become slaves of God," Paul says, "the fruit you get leads to sanctification and its end, eternal life" (v. 22).

Sanctification gets to the very essence of the gospel in the lived-out reality of the daily Christian life. It's what the gospel looks like in the practical existence of the believer. We are already justified but not yet fully glorified (Rom. 8:30). Every child of God pursues Jesus Christ and grows in righteousness daily, and yet every single one of us will reach the end of our life with sins never addressed, mistakes never fixed, and questions never figured out. We do our best to follow God, but we know that our best will fall short. This is the reason for Jesus. Because of him, we can have confidence on the last day that—despite all our shortcomings and mistaken conclusions and even the sin we never noticed and therefore never repented of—God is still our "Father"; we are still God's "sons"; and the kingdom is still our inheritance.

When it comes to gender and sexuality, sanctification means that *all* of us are growing in knowledge of God's law and striving to conform to God's righteousness, even as we know that we will never get it perfectly right. Indeed, straight and cisgender Christians intuitively recognize the need for grace when it comes to sticky questions about gender and sexuality applied to themselves. Few would ever suggest that straight people risk damnation over disagreements about divorce, remarriage, and contraceptive sex. Most Protestants—including some of the most conservative evangelical theologians—reject more fundamentalist approaches to this, preferring grace instead of legalism.[3]

Consider what this means. The Bible "clearly" says that adulterers and the sexually immoral will not inherit the kingdom of heaven, often in the very same passages that Christians use to condemn "homosexuals" (Rom. 1:18–32; 1 Cor. 6:9; 1 Tim. 1:8–11). This means that if straight people *do* answer questions about divorce, remarriage, and contraceptive sex wrong, they would be adulterers and sexual sinners, living in unrepentant sin. Do they risk eternal damnation every time they take a chance on divorce, remarriage, or contraception? Are millions of straight Christians risking their salvation by affirming potentially illicit sex and false marriages? Such a standard spirals into the utterly ridiculous, where no one gets to heaven at all unless they get sexual ethics and gender identity perfectly right. The truth is that all of us will go to our graves with genuine convictions that were still genuinely wrong. None of us will get into heaven having figured out the correct answers to every question we ask about sin.

All of us have our own problems that the Holy Spirit is tackling. This is one reason Jesus told his followers to "take the log out of your own eye" (Matt. 7:5). We should worry about the sin in our *own* lives, instead of trying to condemn others for the sins that look "clear" to us. "Judge not, that you be not judged," Jesus says. "For with the judgment you pronounce you will be judged, and with the measure you use it will be measured to you" (7:1–2). Whatever grace we want for ourselves, we need to be willing to give to others.

14. Grace for Me but Not for Thee

CASEY

Casey attended a Christian academy through high school. In seventh grade, the teacher had students do a report on a well-known historical figure. Casey chose to write about Maya Angelou and referenced Angelou's autobiography, where she speaks candidly about rape and sexual abuse.

"I was scolded by my mom and my teacher for choosing a figure who wrote candidly about her experiences with sexual abuse and the exploration of her own gender and sexual identity," Casey recalled. "For me it really drove home the point that this is something we sweep under the rug."

Not surprisingly, Casey swept her own exploration of sexuality under the rug. "I stopped myself from exploring or even just thinking about how I might feel." In college, a friend came out to her, and she parroted the only words she could think to say. "I told her that I couldn't support her because I don't believe it's right, but the words felt wrong the minute they came out of my mouth."

Eventually, Casey started putting together the pieces of her own sexuality and realized that she was gay. It didn't feel possible. Good Christians weren't supposed to be anything but heterosexual. And yet here she was.

"I worried that I was going to be a disappointment to my family and my friends and also a disappointment to God," Casey recalled. "I really cared what God thought of me. I really cared what this would do to my relationship with him. I didn't want to be separated. I didn't want to be outcast."

Slowly, Casey started coming out, but no one in her Christian community responded well. One of her closest friends told her that "it's absolutely impossible to be a Christian and also be attracted to the same sex" and that Casey "would not be going to heaven."

"She told me that she would pray for me but that she would have to love me from afar," Casey recalled, "and that's the last that I've heard from her in six years."

Casey went to her parents in tears, asking them if they would still be involved in her life if she chose to marry a woman and start a family, and they responded with silence. Another friend met up with Casey and directed the conversation toward homosexuality, informing Casey that she was "going to hell" and that God would not "bless her life" because of her homosexuality.

"It can make you feel like you're not worth being loved," Casey said. "People might say that how I'm loving somebody is wrong. But loving people from 'afar' and making them feel like an outcast? That's not the love that's in the Bible."

■ ■ ■

An uncomfortable disparity exists between how Christians apply the gospel to cisgender, heterosexual people and how they apply it to LGBTQ people. Grace extends to questions about sex, whether related to ethics or gender, only insofar as those questions exist within cisgender, heterosexual marriage. In effect, queer people must enter Christianity fully sanctified. You either do the right thing because you're already saved, or you do the wrong thing because you're not a real Christian in the first place.

Many Christians see nothing wrong with this arrangement. The thinking goes something like this: Would you say that a "murdering Christian" who was proud of being a murderer could be saved? What about a "pedophile Christian" who loves Jesus but also loves molesting children and just wants to be accepted that way? Would you say that a rapist could be a Christian and go on raping? You wouldn't, would you? So why do you think it's okay to say that a gay person can get married or a trans person transition and still be a Christian?

The trouble with this logic is that it presents a false equivalence, conflating sins of conscience with sins of violence. LGBTQ issues are not remotely comparable to murder, rape, and molestation. Queer people don't wrestle with exploiting vulnerable people; they wrestle with how to embody their humanity in a way that is faithful to Jesus. Seeking to understand the boundaries of sexual sin and gender identity is not the same as wanting to violently harm another person.[1]

Most Christians intuit this. Nobody, for example, accuses a pastor of justifying everything from murder to child molestation if he wants to have an honest conversation about whether it's permissible to marry a previously divorced person. People don't respond to questions about contraceptive sex by saying, "But what about the morality of rape?" We know it's challenging to figure out the boundaries of Christian conviction. That doesn't mean we lose all ability to determine right from wrong. It just means that moral questions exist that *are* difficult to figure out and that *do* require grace. Sins of conscience are inherently messy and confusing in ways that most sins of violence are not.

Consider the Bible's condemnations of greed, which exist alongside the Bible's condemnations of "men who bed men." "Do not be deceived," Paul says in 1 Corinthians 6:9–11. "Neither the sexually immoral . . . nor men who practice homosexuality . . . nor the greedy . . . will inherit the kingdom of God." In the previous chapter, he warns the Corinthians to not even associate with someone who is greedy (5:11). Elsewhere, Paul refers to greed, or "covetousness," as "idolatry" (Col. 3:5). In Ephesians 5, he says that "covetous" people have "no inheritance in the kingdom of Christ and God" (v. 5).

These condemnations are clear, and they appear in the same or similar passages as those used to condemn sexual immorality! The Bible treats the sin of greed just as seriously as some of the most fiercely debated issues in the church today. Nevertheless, I've yet to meet a middle-class American Christian who worries about going to hell over their finances. Few Christians in the US would tremble at the possibility of hellfire and brimstone for giving to their retirement accounts instead of giving to the poor or for saving up to go on a family vacation instead of funding a local charity.

Why not? How is it that first-world Christians—who are among the wealthiest people in the history of civilization—have such confidence in their salvation?

The answer is in the meaning of sanctification. If salvation depended on getting our understanding of each and every sin perfectly right, none of us would go to heaven. Struggling to determine the boundaries of a particular sin doesn't condemn you to hell. It makes you a child of God who is learning to be faithful with the life God gives you to live. Navigating morality in a world where Christians are justified but not fully sanctified means learning over *time*. We grow in tandem with the Holy Spirit, discovering the boundaries of righteousness in the *midst* of our walk with God, not before we walk with God. We do our best to learn, but even our best is "like filthy rags" (Isa. 64:6 KJV). When we get to heaven, we're likely to discover that we *all* handled issues of morality in the wrong way, despite our best efforts to the contrary. But that's the point of having a Savior.

Is sin still serious? Of course. God takes sin seriously, and God also gives grace abundantly. Struggling to understand the boundaries of sexual sin doesn't make an LGBTQ person

174

spiritually worse off than it does a cisgender, heterosexual person. It makes both groups of people children of God who are learning to be faithful with the life God gives them to live and the body God gives them to inhabit. The questions that cisgender, heterosexual people ask about their own gender and sexuality might be different from the questions that LGBTQ people ask, but these questions are ultimately cut from the same cloth.

What *if* we get the answers to the questions we ask wrong? God knows the heart of God's people. All of God's children—gay or straight, trans or cis—still belong to Jesus Christ regardless of the filthy rags we offer in our efforts to be righteous. *None* of us will ever be perfect in our understanding of God's law or in our submission to it. *All* of us will arrive at the judgment seat having gotten things wrong about gender and sexuality. That's the point of having a Savior.

I'm reminded of Casey's story. Her good friend said she would love Casey "from afar," believing Casey's sin to be crystal clear. So clear, in fact, that she declared with certainty that Casey "would not be going to heaven." Now, six years later, having never heard from her again, Casey sees the irony of what took place. Her friend was so confident that Casey would go to hell for loving the same sex in the wrong way that she couldn't see how she herself was loving *Casey* in the wrong way.

At the end of the day, LGBTQ Christians are largely asking to be treated with the same grace and good faith that cisgender, heterosexual Christians typically reserve for each other. The question is whether cisgender, heterosexual Christians are willing to share that grace with LGBTQ people. It's possible to create a community defined by the gospel instead of by condemnation. But it takes everyone together. All of us must be willing to give each other the space to grow in tandem with the Holy Spirit.

. . .

You might remember Stephen from the beginning of the book. He's the one who was told to look to Henri Nouwen for inspiration in following Jesus, but the article he read about Nouwen filled him with despair. Celibacy, Stephen told me, was a "wound" that he must choose again and again. He didn't think he could live that way, but he feared that doing otherwise "would be to live in mortal error."

Looking back, Stephen says, "I just wish there had been an acknowledgment from my leaders and community that this was a disputable matter. It would have lifted some of the pressure. It would have been a release valve. If you are reasoning and if you are struggling under the threat of hell, it's not a conducive place to come to an honest opinion."

Stephen survived that period of his life. But years of destructive theological messages and thoughts of suicide left him unable to integrate Christianity into a healthy and flourishing life. "I had to leave Christianity in order to heal," he said. "I don't think it was possible for me to stay and become whole. I just had to leave."

Many Christians hear a story like Stephen's and blame his leaving Christianity on homosexuality. Few consider that perhaps homosexuality was never the issue—that perhaps the church bears responsibility for promoting a theology that Stephen couldn't wrestle with. The fear is that by allowing someone like Stephen to wrestle with sexual ethics, they'll get it wrong and fall into sin. But what if they do?

Every Christian depends on a Jesus whose righteousness covers a multitude of sins, regardless of how far we get in the process of sanctification. This is what it means to be saved. Many Christians claim this righteousness for cisgender, heterosexual people even as they deny it to LGBTQ people. Most don't mean to engage in discrimination, but denying LGBTQ

believers assurance of salvation reflects the prejudices of a
fallen culture.

At the end of the day, it was *Christians* that made Christianity impossible for Stephen. They offered him not the gospel but a legalistic religion where salvation depends on sexual
moralism. "It used to be every waking moment I spent thinking
about my sexuality. The amount of space that it took up, it
wasted away my life for so many years. Now I wake up in the
morning, drink coffee, kiss my partner, and go to work. There
are times that I forget that I'm gay."

Of course, a common charge is that LGBTQ people define
themselves by their gender and sexuality. However, for most
LGBTQ believers, it's the *church* that defines them as such,
forcing them to think about their gender and/or sexuality every
waking moment of every day in order to be good enough Christians. When gay people like Stephen need to *leave* the church
in order to escape being defined by their sexuality, something
is amiss.

Christians made Stephen believe that being miserable as a
gay person was God's will. The Christian life, they explained,
is a "refining fire." "The question is," Stephen told me, "is it a
refining fire or is it a destroying fire?" For Stephen, the expectations of the church nearly destroyed him.

Stephen's story is one of many. And yet, as common as his
story is, it's just as common to find LGBTQ Christians who
don't leave the faith. Who stay and keep trying and keep living
in the midst of a *destroying* fire. Consider Bryan from the last
chapter. He left Christianity after concluding that Jesus didn't
love him. You might remember him telling Jesus, "I want you.
I love you. I need you. But you don't want me, and I can't keep
living this way." He left Christianity in despair, but the Holy
Spirit kept working in his life, and he eventually returned to
Jesus, where he discovered a Savior who not only loved him but
loved him *unconditionally*.

Still, Christians continued to work against the love of God in Bryan's life. He decided to attend seminary, where his room-mates pegged him as being "effeminate." As a joke, they hog-tied his hands and feet together and locked him up in their bedroom closet, leaving him bound and gagged for hours.

Humiliated, Bryan never reported the incident. Instead, he tried to move on, accepting employment at a church while he completed his studies over the next few years. After serving faithfully for a period of time, rumors leaked that he was gay, and within days he was terminated from the ministry. He tried attending a different church, but this church got word from his old church that he was gay. The new pastor contacted Bryan's seminary and informed the leadership that Bryan (who was celibate) was sleeping around with guys. The seminary expelled him a month before graduating with a master's degree.

Of course, not every Christian in Bryan's life has treated him poorly. Several years ago, one of the boys (now grown) who used to beat him up at church reached out to him and apologized in tears for what he had done. Someone else from Bryan's high school also reached out and offered a similar apology. Bryan explained to me that he won't ever be able to be friends with either of them, but their genuine grief and repentance brought him a degree of healing.

As a result of these conflicting and traumatic experiences, Bryan's relationship to the church remains complicated even as he holds onto his faith. Recently, he ran into another one of the Christian boys from his high school who tied him to a tree and beat him nearly unconscious. Hoping that perhaps this man's heart might have changed like the other two men, Bryan asked him if he regretted what he had done. The man replied, "Hell, no. You're a f—ing f-g."

Few Christians would outright condone such behavior, and yet Bryan's experience demonstrates that such behavior is com-mon among Christians nevertheless. Why would hatred flourish among people who believe in God's love? Why do LGBTQ people find themselves fighting against Christians, of all people, to follow Jesus?

At the heart of the problem is a culture that denies LGBTQ people the gospel. Whenever Christians fail to give other believers the grace they claim for themselves, they fail to embody the love of Jesus Christ, giving purchase to hate. At a fundamental level, many assume that LGBTQ people are going to hell unless they approach difficult questions about gender and sexuality correctly. This automatically creates a context for prejudice and discrimination, regardless of people's intent. Not everyone would tell a gay person, "You're a f—ing f-g," but when Christians make salvation for LGBTQ people contingent on sex and gender, the effect is much the same. The end result is that people who *do* say such things find cover in a theology they can easily use to justify their bigotry.

BURDEN 7 SUMMARY

We thus conclude the seventh burden that LGBTQ people bear in the church. Grace extends to questions about gender and sexuality only insofar as those questions exist within cisgender, heterosexual marriage. This means that any question that an LGBTQ person might ask about sexual ethics and gender identity risks their eternal salvation. LGBTQ people must get it right from the start or go to hell.

A BETTER WAY

15. Recentering the Gospel

The year was 1525. Balthasar Hubmaier took Ulrich Zwingli to task in a public debate over the merits of infant baptism. Both were leaders of the Reformation, but the debate took place in Zwingli's hometown of Zurich, where Zwingli's influence held sway. In humiliating fashion, Hubmaier quoted prior statements by Zwingli in which Zwingli—who had become a strident defender of infant baptism—admitted that no scriptural support existed for infant baptism.

Enraged and embarrassed, Zwingli had Hubmaier thrown into prison and tortured. Four months later, he authorized the execution of anyone who practiced believer's baptism. Hubmaier managed to escape but was burned at the stake two years later. Hubmaier's wife had a millstone tied around her neck and was drowned in the Danube River.[1]

It was only the beginning of what would become centuries of conflict between Protestants who practiced *infant* baptism and Protestants who practiced *believer's* baptism. Those who practiced infant baptism fell back on the traditional perspective of the church, teaching that God's covenant to his chosen people included the children who were born to them. Those who practiced believer's baptism taught what was seen as a dangerous new theology, preaching that baptism ought to be administered only after a person professed *knowing* faith in Jesus Christ.

At the time, the vast majority of the most influential Protestant figures defended infant baptism, including Luther and Calvin. Believer's baptism was considered a fringe (even extremist) belief, and Christians who practiced it faced unrelenting persecution. They were whipped, excommunicated, fined, imprisoned, drowned, tortured, and, in the aftermath of the Anabaptist Münster Rebellion, massacred by the hundreds in a sectarian conflict that featured radicalism on both sides.[2] As late as the eighteenth century, Baptist congregations in the United States were still meeting in secret, kept trapdoors in their meeting rooms, and planted lookouts in the trees to alert congregants of danger.[3]

The violent and bloody history attached to Protestant beliefs about baptism is hard to fathom today. In the twenty-first century, a baby-baptizing Presbyterian Church in America (PCA) pastor and a believer-baptizing Southern Baptist pastor can speak at the same conference and get lunch together without anyone ending up dead. But at one point in time, Christians were killing each other over baptism, and they believed they were defending the gospel when they did it.

Learning from History

For many Christians, one of the hardest ideas to swallow is that someone can affirm same-sex marriage and still be Christian. *How is that possible?* they ask. *The progressive definition of marriage and the traditional definition of marriage are simply incompatible. One definition is scriptural. The other is not. There's no way we could possibly get along as siblings in Christ. I could never call them a fellow believer.*

But we already have precedent for resolving theological differences of similar magnitude. Baptism is no small deal. It gets to the heart of how we think about the unfolding of God's covenant in the pages of Scripture, what it means to be a member of the family of God, what we believe about salvation, and how we think about Christian identity. It's for this reason that the Nicene Creed assents to "one baptism" for the forgiveness of sins and only one. It's also the reason why defenders of one kind of baptism condemned anyone who practiced the other as heretics. Those who adhere to infant baptism approach the Bible in drastically different ways than those who adhere to believer's baptism.

Unlike marriage, baptism and the Lord's Supper remain sacraments in Protestant denominations. Even so, we now largely understand that a member of the Southern Baptist Church and a member of the PCA are siblings in Christ, even despite differences of *sacramental* significance. Few people today would measure someone's salvation by whether they baptize their babies. Indeed, we look upon that era of Christian history with a degree of embarrassment. We talk about it so little that many have forgotten.

Centuries later, we now face theological differences of similar magnitude over sex, marriage, and gender. Some people might argue that these issues are incomparable because marriage is a symbol of Christ and the church. However, to borrow Calvin, mustard seeds symbolize the church too—as does friendship and sonship and many other analogies. Baptism itself is considered a "sign and seal" of God's covenant. Scripture relies on a wealth of imagery to convey the mystery of the gospel and our relationship to God. Marriage doesn't have a monopoly on this. Is it an important institution? Absolutely yes. Is it a covenant before God with tremendous moral consequence? Again, yes. But in our haste to affirm the significance of marriage, we must not make it more essential to the Christian faith than it is. It's important, yes, but if we can differ in our understanding of baptism and other sacraments, certainly we can differ in our understanding of marriage.

Some would argue that sex, marriage, and gender are different from baptism because they touch upon our understanding of sin. And yet, even here, Christians *still* get along. Those who practice believer's baptism believe that Christians baptized as infants (and never baptized again) ignore a core mandate of Jesus Christ. From this perspective, such Christians are living in sin. Those who practice infant baptism, on the other hand, believe that those who refuse to baptize infants are denying children an essential means of grace. From this perspective, such parents are living in sin too.

Nevertheless, most of us still respect each other as siblings in Christ. We recognize that the gospel is more essential to our faith than such differences, even differences over doctrinal matters with tremendous moral consequence. I'm reminded of John Piper's willingness to give grace for Christians to divorce and remarry even though he believes this practice is adulterous. If we recognize that straight people need this kind of grace, why not gay people too?

Living in Contrast instead of Conflict

We've already arrived at a place where Christians of all stripes believe different things about gender and sexuality. However, we've not yet arrived at a place where we do so in the Spirit of peace, love, and unity that ought to characterize Christian differences. Same-sex marriage and gender identity cause denominational schisms, split families, and ruin lives, with LGBTQ people caught in the cross fire. We can't keep going this way.

It's time to lay down our weapons and put an end to this battle. The fact is, when we get to heaven, we might be surprised by who we share the kingdom of God with: Old Testament patriarchs who practiced polygamy, New Testament women who engaged in prostitution, contemporary couples who got divorced and remarried multiple times, and LGBTQ people whose every choice and every breath was subject to scrutiny.

As long as LGBTQ people are the rope in a never-ending tug-of-war between progressives and traditionalists, LGBTQ people will suffer and the entire church along with them. It's time to find a better approach. Differences of Christian belief and practice related to sex, marriage, and gender aren't going away. That doesn't mean we disagree on the essentials of the Christian faith. The ancient creeds exist for a reason. Christianity doesn't rise and fall over our beliefs about sexual ethics and gender identity any more than it does over believer's baptism versus infant baptism. Or the Lord's Supper. Or spiritual gifts. Or numerous other disputes.

In the end, we must learn to embody our convictions in a way that is faithful to the Holy Spirit's witness in our lives without denying the work of the Holy Spirit in the lives of other people. A friend from my alma mater, Mary Sue Daoud, put it to me this way: we can live in contrast to each other without living in conflict with each other. We don't always need to oppose perspectives that don't fall in line with our own. Living at peace with our faith doesn't require combat.

Don't get me wrong. There's a time and place for opposition. But there's also a time and place for cooperation. And when it comes to gender and sexuality, I think it's time we learned to cooperate. We can live in diversity without living in animosity. We can do our best to be faithful to the witness of Scripture while affirming the best efforts of our siblings in Christ to also be faithful to the witness of Scripture. Their best is no better than ours. All of our works are like filthy rags (Isa. 64:6).

A Simple Idea

With all this in mind, I want us to consider a simple possibility moving forward: give LGBTQ people space to navigate questions about gender and sexuality regardless of the convictions that others might have about the same questions in their own lives. Are some convictions worth drawing lines in the sand to identify who is Christian and who is not? Undoubtedly. But celibacy, same-sex marriage, and gender identity aren't among them.

I mentioned the church's violent and bloody history attached to baptism because it's important to remember that Christians have learned how to co-exist as siblings in Christ even for some of the most hotly contested doctrines of the Christian faith. Things like baptism and the Lord's Supper are about as major as it gets when it comes to theology. But we've nevertheless figured out a way to affirm each other's faith despite our differences.

At the same time, denominationalism isn't necessarily the solution when it comes to debates over sexual ethics and gender identity. These debates are different in that they involve the stigmatization of a person's *humanity*, not just their theology. If society, with the help of Christians, had never created the category of "homosexuality" in the first place, we'd be having a different conversation. But that's not what happened. The stigma attached to psychopathological categories continues to haunt LGBTQ people. This means we can't solve our problems by segregating into denominations based on our theology of sex and gender. Such practices are now inextricably caught up in the exclusion of LGBTQ people as *people*.

Indeed, membership criteria that require adherence to the heterosexual definition of marriage and the essentialist definition of gender have a long history of abuse toward LGBTQ people. As a result, attaching such requirements to church membership, even if done with good intentions, communicates to LGBTQ people that their belonging is conditional—that Christians are happy to cast them out the minute they don't get in line. This type of approach only deepens long-standing wounds. Church leaders may intend to merely clarify doctrine, but in so doing, they communicate to queer people that *they* are not wanted as *people*. It's unrealistic to expect queer people to no longer feel injured by practices that Christians have historically used to kick them out. Healing such wounds requires a radically different approach.

This can sound daunting, especially for people who come from a traditional perspective on sexual ethics, but it's not impossible. Bill Henson, for example, leads a Christian organization extending Christ's love to LGBTQ people. His training, called Posture Shift, provides guidance to ministry leaders from a traditional perspective on sexual ethics. I heard him speak for the first time in 2019 at Revoice, where he presented a "missiological" model, walking Christians through an approach to inclusion that doesn't predicate church membership upon LGBTQ marital status or gender identity. Some churches might balk at this idea, and Henson is quick to say that he would never tell a pastor to officiate a wedding if doing so would violate their church's theology. Nor does he ask churches to change their leadership requirements. He does note, however, that "you cannot reach banished people for Christ by banishing them."

Indeed, LGBTQ people have *already* been cast out. Policies that empower Christians to continue kicking them out of their churches only make the problem worse. We need churches that are implementing policies and practices designed to *invite* LGBTQ people *into* the body of Christ as full members, regardless of the questions they have and the answers they find. Years of exclusionary practices require *inclusionary* practices to fully correct. Henson puts it this way:

> We want folks to experience increased family acceptance and enhanced church inclusion. Why? Because it's the only way to nourish faith identity. Every missionary around the world knows you don't go to a marginalized people group and then start demanding urgent things of them. You go to a marginalized people group and you take a posture of humility, listening,

learning, creating safety, inviting, offering hospitality, and bringing Jesus close to them where they are as they are. It's called
proximity. Every missionary understands without proximity
there is no advancement of the gospel in human hearts, particularly when you're encountering marginalized people who
have already been wounded by people like us.[4]

Henson's challenge has stuck with me. When it comes to
LGBTQ issues, exclusionary policies communicate to LGBTQ
people that they cannot access life-giving faith unless they agree
to a particular definition of marriage and gender. This is not
the gospel. It only perpetuates condemnation.

Even more, I wonder if we can imagine a future where churches
see the question of same-sex marriage and gender identity as
important, yes, but not ultimate. Might it be possible to build a
future where we distinguish between matters of sexual violence
and matters of sexual conscience? Might we tighten our grip on
things like rape, assault, and abuse even as we make space for differences of belief on the definition of marriage? Might it be possible to allow LGBTQ people to even hold positions of leadership
in churches regardless of their marital status and gender identity?

I believe it is.

Right now, we have it backward. We have a culture where
people like Andy Savage sexually assault young girls under their
leadership, confess their "sin," and remain ordained as of the
writing of this book. Meanwhile, gay people merely questioning their sexuality get kicked out of their churches. It doesn't
have to be this way.

It's time for this to change.

16. Setting Down the Burdens

Most Christians don't *mean* to hurt anyone when they adopt harmful approaches toward LGBTQ issues. Quite the opposite. Most want to help. Many Christians see telling the truth in love as a Christian duty. They want to disciple LGBTQ people in the Christian faith and encourage them to stay the course in their walk with Jesus.

At the same time, in their well-intended efforts, many Christians leave problematic assumptions about gender and sexuality unexamined, causing their solutions to perpetuate attitudes toward LGBTQ people that inflict real and lasting damage. Rarely do I meet a Christian who actually intends to hurt people. But allowing hurtful assumptions to drive our solutions inevitably does harm, even when we mean to do well.

At the beginning of this book, I introduced LGBTQ discrimination as a "totalizing system" in the church. We often think of discrimination as individual acts that harm other people and only as individual acts. While it's true that discrimination *does* take the form of hurtful words and actions, those hurtful words and actions wouldn't exist apart from the attitudes, norms, and power structures from which they emerge. Getting struck by lightning might kill you, but the lightning didn't cause itself. There's a much bigger thunderstorm blocking out the sun, making the wind, rain, and lightning possible.

In wide swaths of the church, there's a storm system blocking out the gospel. The pain and trauma experienced by LGBTQ people wouldn't be possible otherwise. That storm system looks like a theological milieu in which all the preceding burdens churn and swirl in different churches and denominations, creating the context in which LGBTQ people simply cannot access life-giving Christianity.

Taken altogether, many Christians consistently preach and believe that celibacy is unnatural even as they simultaneously push celibacy onto gay people (Burden 1). Many Christians further offer marriage as the solution to sexual attraction even as they simultaneously expect gay people to only marry the gender they *don't* find sexually attractive (also Burden 1). Many Christians say that identity should be found in Christ even as they push a narrative onto LGBTQ people that labels them pathological "sinners" (Burden 2). Worse, many Christians consistently fall back on politicized tropes in which LGBTQ people symbolize everything Christians ought to stand against (Burden 3).

When LGBTQ people question this treatment, many Christians expend tremendous energy protecting the existence of words like *homosexual* and *homosexuality* in modern translations of Scripture in order to respond that the Bible is "clear" (Burden 4). Having tossed the complexity of Scripture aside, many Christians then force upon queer people an arbitrary system of gender roles and expectations that is simply inaccessible to many, if not most, LGBTQ people (Burden 5). Worse, many Christians adopt the secular philosophy of gender essentialism with precious little debate or consideration, reducing trans and intersex people to their sexual biology and nothing more, as if this were a faithful expression of the *imago Dei* (Burden 6).

Huddled outside in the wind and rain, LGBTQ Christians stare *inside* at churches filled with cisgender, heterosexual people whose theology has evolved over the past five hundred years to accommodate their needs and desires, producing a heterosexual definition of marriage (Burdens 1 and 4) and a deterministic definition of gender (Burdens 5 and 6) that few would recognize in the two-thousand-year history of the faith. And yet LGBTQ people are told that believing in this system is not just biblical but ultimately essential to go to heaven (Burden 7).

Of course, not every Christian agrees with everything I just described. Many, in fact, feel deeply uncomfortable with the way things are, recognizing the undue burden that all the above creates for LGBTQ people. And yet what I've described is still the way things are in too many contexts.

These burdens do harm because they depend on a belief system built for cisgender, heterosexual Christians to the exclusion of everyone else. That doesn't make cisgender, heterosexual Christians bad people. It just means that change is necessary. If you've made it this far, it's likely because you're already wrestling with how to make things better. At the end of the day, as long as heterosexism and cissexism are attached to differences of belief about sexual ethics and gender identity, it will be impossible to create healthy churches where *all* people can thrive. A truly biblical approach to gender and sexuality will be good for *all* people in the church, not just for some.

With that in mind, let's walk through the issues together and think about next steps in relation to the burdens I've named.

Reject Mandatory Lifelong Celibacy

It's time to rethink our assumptions about human sexuality, particularly the idea that lifelong celibacy is impossible and that marriage is the answer to lust. These beliefs undergird a host of problems in the church, including the idea that sexual frustration inevitably leads to sin unless you get married, that women are responsible for male lust, that the only answer to lust is sex, and that rape and sexual abuse are merely the result of caving to sexual temptation. With ongoing allegations of sexual abuse in the church multiplying by the day, Christians have little hope of addressing the crisis if they don't reevaluate their assumptions about human sexuality, starting here.

However, that doesn't mean we need to go back to the way things were. Reformers might have been mistaken in many ways, but they also had valuable insight. When it comes to sexuality, they correctly identified that mandatory lifelong celibacy is bad spiritual practice. The reasons they offered might have been problematic, but the observation is valid. *Forcing* people to be celibate forever doesn't work.

The reason is that celibacy turns into legalism unless experienced as a positive *response* to one's faith as we walk in relationship with Jesus instead of a coercive *requirement* in order to be in relationship with Jesus in the first place. This doesn't mean that we don't have convictions that we hold with deep commitment. Instead, it means that convictions requiring celibacy or marriage to a gender we don't find attractive ought to be a yardstick for *ourselves*, not others. A path with such profound, lifelong consequences needs to be experienced as a product of freedom and not of bondage.

Furthermore, it's time to build a church where celibacy is not only a choice but also a choice that is livable, something that is not only respected but also desirable as a vocation. This means developing alternative ways of doing family and community apart from marriage. Too many churches offer marriage as the only solution to sexual desire and the nuclear family as the only way to experience relational intimacy. At the end of the day, if churches want people to choose celibacy as a legitimate Christian vocation, doing so shouldn't relegate people to loneliness for the rest of their lives. Loneliness is not a vocation. It's time to broaden our understanding of Christian community to include pathways for love, intimacy, and relational connectedness outside of marriage and the nuclear family.

For myself, as I've journeyed with Jesus, I've found a traditional approach to sexual ethics to be compelling and am celibate as a result. In addition, because I experience celibacy as a positive calling in response to my relationship with Jesus—a relationship that my sex life cannot jeopardize, celibate or not—I've also found celibacy to be life-giving. That doesn't give me the right to legislate my journey upon the rest of the church. To borrow the words of Luther, "Why should another's holiness disturb my liberty? Why should another's zeal take me captive?"[1] Or in my case, why should my *own* pursuit of holiness take *other* people captive? Christian liberty applies to cisgender and heterosexual people when it comes to questions of similar magnitude. LGBTQ people deserve the same grace. Do some ethical questions merit enforcement? Of course. But mandatory lifelong celibacy isn't one of them.

Celebrate Queerness as an Avenue of Grace

If Christians only talked about heterosexuality in the context of sin, we could easily conclude that heterosexuality is the opposite of holiness. In fact, after a long conversation in which we detailed every new case of sexual assault committed by straight people, pornography use, fornication, adultery, promiscuity, divorce, and the like, we might go so far as to say that straight people must renounce heterosexuality altogether. Indeed, this is how far medieval Roman Catholicism went in the years leading up to the Reformation. It led to rampant corruption and Draconian control over marriage and sexuality.

But defining human sexuality by sin doesn't work and never will. It creates a context where sin becomes inescapable, robbing people of a soteriology defined by the righteousness of

Jesus Christ. If straight and cisgender people can pursue holiness but still be straight and cisgender, then LGBTQ people can also pursue holiness and still be LGBTQ. Whenever Christians permanently attach sin to the queer experience, they make queer people especially sinful in ways that straight and cisgender people are not.

It's therefore time to "reorient" the way Christians think about queerness. We need to shift our thinking away from fear of sin and, instead, celebrate the uniquely queer ways that LGBTQ people walk in faithfulness to Jesus. Do queer people sin? Of course. Do they sometimes sin in ways that differ from straight and cisgender people? Once again, of course. But being gay is no more sinful because a gay person sins in *gay* ways than being straight is sinful because a straight person sins in *straight* ways. Both are fallen because both are *human*, but both can also be avenues of grace—because both are *human*. It's time to celebrate the ways in which LGBTQ people experience queerness as an avenue of grace.

But what if I believe that gay sex is a sin? Plenty of gay people experience their sexuality in ways that produce faithfulness to Jesus outside the boundaries of sex and marriage. About half of the stories featured in this book are from queer people who pursue celibacy. *Even if* you believe that gay sex is a sin, this belief is not a valid reason to define gay sexuality by sin. Sex is not the defining feature of what it means to be gay. There's more to the experience of sexuality than just sex, and there's more to the experience of *gayness* in particular than just sex.

No matter what Christians believe about sex, it's time to shift the conversation away from sin and, instead, celebrate the ways in which LGBTQ believers experience their queerness as an avenue of grace. When we obsess over sin, we define people by sin. When we obsess over grace, we finally see the ways that God is at work in creation. It's time to obsess over grace in the queer experience.

Repent of Abuses and Engage in Learning Opportunities

LGBTQ people remain demonized in countless Christian communities, often evoking fear, hatred, resentment, disgust, and even violent rage. On top of that, they get blamed for just about anything that goes wrong in our culture, especially if it's connected to gender and sexuality. As a result, Christians end up fighting a queer phantom that will supposedly destroy the church even as they ignore myriad other problems that actually afflict Christian communities.

It's therefore time to dismantle the "folk devil" myth. Churches need to work toward a future where "gay" and "Christian" are not seen as contradictions. The same can be said of every other LGBTQ term. This means giving queer believers greater visibility in the church, including positions of leadership where they can be fully out as both queer and Christian. It also means letting LGBTQ people serve in children's and youth ministry. Instead of relying on prejudice, churches need to rely on research-backed practices that protect children and ensure that all adults, regardless of gender and orientation, are fit to work with minors. (It's also worth repeating that most predators are cisgender and heterosexual.)

In addition, it's time to acknowledge the role Christians have played in the mistreatment of LGBTQ people, not just historically but up to the present day. Collective Christian fear of and resentment toward LGBTQ people is first and foremost a product of sin. It won't go away until Christians confess and repent and seek to do better. This can be done by engaging proactively with LGBTQ advocacy groups, hosting trainings and workshops for church leaders as well as congregants, publicly correcting false narratives about queer people, and creating space in churches for queer people to experience acceptance regardless of marital status or gender identity.

It's further crucial that churches clearly and explicitly explain their beliefs, practices, and policies surrounding LGBTQ issues. Many LGBTQ believers attend churches faithfully only to find themselves unexpectedly barred from membership, leadership, volunteer opportunities, and more. It can feel like a "bait and switch," and it leaves many suspicious when churches don't clearly state their positions in easy-to-find locations. Regardless of where churches stand in their approach to LGBTQ issues, it's crucial to be publicly honest.

Give LGBTQ Christians Space to Ask Questions and Consider Possibilities

Insisting that the Bible is "clear" on LGBTQ issues when, in fact, it's pretty complicated is one of the church's greatest failures of the past century. It has led to an almost zealous commitment to modern categories like "homosexuality" existing in Scripture and an overreliance on proof-texting. Christians typically engage in proof-texting in order to demonstrate that the Bible is "clear." But instead of proving biblical clarity, this merely pulls competing scholars into esoteric debates about the Greek and Hebrew language, further demonstrating that the Bible is anything but "clear" when it comes to gender and sexuality.

It's therefore time to give LGBTQ Christians space to ask questions, wrestle with Scripture, and make sense out of the biblical narrative. False notions of the "obvious" create an atmosphere where questions are unacceptable. Following Scripture becomes a matter of "getting in line" as opposed to understanding God's Word. It's impossible to engage in authentic pursuit of God's truth when fallen human beings (who think they know God's truth) determine the only right answer from the get-go. Intellectually honest inquiry results only when people can wrestle with even taboo answers to the questions they raise. It's time to make space for questions, and it's time to allow for discussion.

If you'd like to gain a better appreciation for how LGBTQ Christians are helping to clarify and make sense out of sexual ethics, whether progressive or traditional, check out the following books:

Books by authors who affirm same-sex marriage

Scripture, Ethics, and the Possibility of Same-Sex Relationships by Karen Keen

Bible, Gender, Sexuality by James Brownson

Beyond Shame by Matthias Roberts

God and the Gay Christian by Matthew Vines

Torn by Justin Lee

Walking the Bridgeless Canyon by Kathy Baldock

Books by authors who follow traditional ethics

Guiding Families of LGBT+ Loved Ones by Bill Henson

Single, Gay, Christian by Greg Coles

Oriented to Faith by Tim Otto

All but Invisible by Nate Collins

Spiritual Friendship by Wesley Hill

Gay and Catholic by Eve Tushnet

Make Room for Gender Expressions That Don't Fit the Cultural Script

Pagan assumptions about gender and its relationship to power have dominated Western Christian thinking for too long, contributing to homophobic stereotypes about effeminate "fags" and masculine "dykes." Such stereotypes function to reinforce Eurocentric gender norms by shaming anyone who doesn't fit in. Christian maturity thereby transforms into an arbitrary performance of gender, disproportionately impacting not only LGBTQ people but also women and people of color. At the end of the day, this gender performance tells us nothing about a person's Christian maturity.

Many Christians feel the need to delineate in explicit ways exactly how men and women "of God" ought to look, sound, and behave. This attachment to reductionistic definitions inevitably forces many LGBTQ people into boxes that don't fit. Does the Word of God provide instructions for how to live a holy life? Certainly. But pursuing holiness is not the same thing as conforming to cultural expressions of gender.

It's therefore time for Christians to get comfortable with people who challenge the boxes. This means acknowledging the masculinity of so-called effeminates as well as the femininity of so-called dykes. It also means celebrating the humanity of people who don't fit into either category of masculine or feminine. At the end of the day, if human beings are made in the image of God, then human beings will also be bigger than the boxes our culture creates.

Adopt a Posture of Humility

My book can't prove to readers that trans women are women or that trans men are men. Like the debate over same-sex marriage, other books engage that conversation better than I could. Instead, my book is merely asking readers to reconsider what we assume to be true about the relationship between sex and gender.

The idea that sex determines gender, otherwise known as gender essentialism, is a concept deeply rooted in paganism, leading to an approach to human identity that encourages hypersexualization, reducing men and women to gender roles defined by sexual biology and nothing more. Quoting prooftexts and repeating that "God made them male and female" isn't enough to address the problematic anthropology that essentialism entails.

It's therefore time to adopt a posture of humility when it comes to the relationship between sex and gender. It's time to be okay with saying, "I don't know." It's time to admit that the predominant approach doesn't work.

Some readers might find it frustrating that I don't define gender in the pages of this book, but it's our obsession with defining gender that created this mess in the first place. Maybe it's time to sit in the discomfort of not having answers. Maybe it's time to embrace the *mystery* of gender instead of trying to explain it.

At the very least, it's time to learn from trans and intersex people and to prioritize their health and well-being above casting moral judgments on something that none of us fully comprehend. This means believing a person when they tell us their gender instead of assuming that you or I or a microscope in a lab know better what their gender ought to be. It means using the pronouns that people tell us to use and, ultimately, taking a step back to understand them. Most importantly, it means learning from the trans and intersex community instead of learning from those who merely reinforce our prior beliefs.

This can be hard. It means setting aside our fears and prejudices in order to listen to a group of people that most Christians, until now, have done a poor job of listening to. It means taking the time to learn and educate ourselves on a topic that none of us fully understand. Below are some books to get started:

Transforming: The Bible and the Lives of Transgender Christians by Austen Hartke

Trans-Gender: Theology, Ministries, and Communities of Faith by Justin Sabia-Tanis

Sex Difference in Christian Theology: Male, Female, and Intersex in the Image of God by Megan K. DeFranza

Everything You Ever Wanted to Know about Trans (But Were Afraid to Ask) by Brynn Tannehill

I Know What Heaven Looks Like: A Modern Day Coming of Age Story by Lawrence Richardson

Affirm LGBTQ Christians as Equal Heirs to the Kingdom

It's time to let go of the idea that what LGBTQ people believe about sexual ethics and gender identity somehow determines their eternal destination. As long as Christians preach a gospel where the only questions that are allowed to be asked about gender and sexuality are cisgender and heterosexual questions, then Christians are preaching a gospel where people need to be straight and cisgender in order to be assured of salvation. This is not the gospel.

What does it look like for LGBTQ people to follow Jesus faithfully with their gender and sexuality? Should they be celibate? Should they marry the same sex? Should they marry the opposite sex? Is it okay to identify as gay or trans or queer? Is it okay to live as a different gender than the gender assigned at birth? What is the relationship between sex and gender? Is there a relationship at all?

LGBTQ Christians arrive at different answers to all of these questions. Regardless, they deserve space to work out these questions without the pressure of eternal damnation ever looming in the background. It's time to let go of threatening LGBTQ people with hell and damnation for answering questions about celibacy, same-sex marriage, and gender identity "wrong." Nobody's salvation hinges on getting these questions "right." Our salvation hinges on the *saving* work of Jesus Christ and him alone. It's therefore time to affirm LGBTQ Christians as equal heirs to the kingdom of God, regardless of their marital status, gender identity, or commitment to lifelong celibacy.

17. Weights of Glory

It would be a mistake to conclude from my book that the LGBTQ experience is defined only by trauma and unhappiness. While my book is largely dedicated to unpacking the things that lead to trauma, depression, anxiety, and suicidal thoughts among LGBTQ people in the church, the story doesn't end here. I've focused on the cause of these problems because too many Christians remain unaware of the real issues that sexual and gender minorities face. Fixing a problem means first understanding what is causing the problem. My book is designed to help people understand the contribution that we, the church, have made to the problems that exist today, something that most discussions lack.

However, LGBTQ Christians aren't a bunch of tragic, hopeless victims. Faced with a world that often rejects them, many LGBTQ believers build their own communities and find their own ways of flourishing regardless of acceptance or condemnation. LGBTQ Christians have experienced hardship, yes, but they are also actively creating pathways to heal from those experiences and follow Jesus regardless of the persecution they face.

You might remember Jonah. He's the one who lost his job at a Christian youth camp after coming out as gay and celibate. He went to his church for support, but many were too busy debating whether Jonah was a pedophile, arguing that he was living in sin for identifying as "gay" instead of "same-sex attracted" and campaigning to permanently bar same-sex-attracted people from serving in youth ministry. We left Jonah contemplating suicide, sitting at his desk with a bottle of wine and ninety-six pills at his fingertips. But Jonah didn't die that day. As he wrestled with suicidal thoughts, a voice spoke to him in that moment, telling him to give the pills to a friend. So he did. In the days thereafter, he decided to do what was necessary to save his life, and he left his church as a result. Some Christians might look at Jonah's choice to leave as a failure on his part. But for Jonah it was a matter of survival. "I almost walked away from the faith altogether. I was burned so hard. I didn't want to get burned again."

Jonah now attends a church where he can be gay and Christian apart from scrutiny. Better yet, he filed a formal complaint with the university that managed the Christian camp that fired him, and over the span of a year, he successfully lobbied for the camp to change course. The following summer, he was reinstated at his job.

Jonah's experience is an important reminder that our lives are characterized not only by struggle but also by triumph. The valley of the shadow of death is only one part of a journey that also includes green pastures and goodness and mercy (Ps. 23). However dark our lives may be right now, it *does* get better.[1] In the lowest of our lows, the enemy feeds us a lie that this is the way it will be for the rest of our days, that there is no escape, only death. But this has never been true and will never be true.

Jonah's story is not over and will certainly include more ups and downs. But what strikes me most about Jonah's story (and every other story in this book) is that Christians were the greatest obstacle to his faith. We might find inspiration in stories like Jonah's, where believers overcome persecution, but Christians of all people shouldn't be the source of that persecution.

204

Many LGBTQ people find it necessary to create their own faith communities, not as a means to distance themselves from other believers but as a means of survival. These communities become sacred pathways for LGBTQ people to experience the love of Jesus Christ and life-giving faith.

Indeed, LGBTQ people call each other "family" because that's what we are to each other in a world that rejects us. Among LGBTQ believers, that bond is especially strong because it originates in the unity we share through Jesus Christ, a spiritual family that transcends the boundaries of a world that is passing away. A gospel community.

In my own life, the first time I ever attended a majority queer church pastored by a lesbian, I was ready to catch heresy behind every word and every whisper. Instead, I heard the gospel, and I heard it time and again, in more detail and with more depth and conviction than I had heard from the pulpit in years. It occurred to me that this is what so many churches have lost in their battles over sex and gender. We've lost sight of the good news of Jesus Christ. However important marriage is and however consequential sexual ethics are to the way we live our daily lives, they cannot and should not replace the primacy of the gospel message.

Jesus told his followers, "By this all people will know that you are my disciples, if you have love for one another" (John 13:35). The problem is that many Christians *tell* LGBTQ people "I love you" even as their love feels unrecognizable to anyone who has ever loved or *been* loved before. I'm reminded of Casey, whose friend politely informed her that she would love her "from afar" and never spoke to her again.

Underneath such encounters is the felt knowledge that, however much Christians *tell* LGBTQ people "I love you," many LGBTQ people in the church are not actually loved. When Christian "love" looks eerily similar to self-righteousness, bigotry, and prejudice, it's no surprise that LGBTQ people question what the church is about.

Of course, many Christians worry that LGBTQ believers are replacing the gospel with an amorphous, wishy-washy "luhv" that just lets people do whatever they want regardless of sin and theological truth. In reality, however, I know few people who take sin and theological truth as seriously as LGBTQ Christians. People might disagree with where different LGBTQ believers land theologically when it comes to sexual ethics and gender identity, but I know few people who spend as much time as queer believers in searching Scripture for God's revealed will on these topics. Many spend years and even decades studying the Bible, going to seminary, reading books by theologians from all sides, and weeping over the pages of Scripture. They do so because they desire to follow Jesus and arrive at an understanding of sexual ethics and gender identity that is faithful to God's Word. Far from following their feelings or the tides of cultural change, they want to submit to God's will.

LGBTQ Christians vary across the spectrum of theological convictions. The temptation is to assume that whichever LGBTQ people happen to agree with our *own* convictions are the ones who did the *real* theological work. But intelligent people with genuine faith exist on all sides of the spectrum and come to different conclusions on these topics even as they are nevertheless driven by the same genuine desire to submit to God's law.

You might remember Meredith, who faced layers of challenges associated with not only being a queer Black woman but also being married to a white man. It was neither her marriage nor her sexuality nor her race that was the issue but rather the stigma of failing to fit in the boxes of fallen culture. Some might stereotype Meredith as an overbearing feminist liberal for the egalitarian gender dynamic that exists in her marriage. However, at the same time, Meredith holds to a traditional understanding of sexual ethics. She believes marriage to be a union between one man and one woman, and she attends a conservative church in the PCA. She told me that if she were convicted differently about sexual ethics in Scripture, she might have married a woman. But because her own study of Scripture led her to a traditional perspective, she's chosen a different path, a path that works for her *and* allows her to live at peace with her convictions.

Some people who don't share Meredith's beliefs might say that she's repressed. Such stereotypes fail to grapple with the complexities of resolving one's sexuality in light of one's faith. LGBTQ Christians need to find healthy ways to understand their sexuality, yes, but without a means to do so in light of their religious beliefs, many will conclude that they cannot be queer and Christian. This alone is enough to drive many LGBTQ Christians to suicide. If Meredith's journey brings her to traditional convictions about sex and marriage, marrying a woman isn't the answer. It would just make her feel conflicted and guilty and pit her faith against her marriage. Some might be tempted to mock Meredith's convictions or call it "self-hating," but mocking accomplishes little. People like Meredith already experience marginalization. They don't need further shame. Instead, they need support as they build a life that allows them to live at peace with their faith and thrive in relational wholeness.

Indeed, LGBTQ people who share Meredith's convictions, like me, pursue a host of relational possibilities not limited to heterosexual marriage. These pathways include chosen family, intentional community, and even partnership (because marriage is not the only option for covenant relationships). We often face myriad challenges as we attempt to carve out ways to do community outside the confines of sex and marriage, and we need just as much support as anyone else in the queer community.

At the same time, not all queer believers share Meredith's convictions. Many are questioning their beliefs and actively exploring what it might look like to follow traditional teaching, and they remain open to the possibility of other theological positions. Their questions aren't a threat, and they aren't a sign of temptation. Questioning is a natural part of trying to make sense out of God's will, and it's something that all Christians do throughout their lives.

Many other LGBTQ Christians arrive at theological conclusions that don't require gay celibacy or heterosexual marriage. You might remember Jack, whose church performed several exorcisms on them in an attempt to rebuke the "homosexual" demons that possessed them. After suffering a major stroke, Jack began a process of searching to find better answers than what church after church had been telling Jack they needed to believe but with little rationale. This process led Jack to affirm not only same-sex marriage but also their gender fluidity and feminine expression.

Many might dismiss someone like Jack as caving to their sinful desires and twisting God's Word to their liking. Jack moves easily in theological debates on many topics and can run circles around most pastors in discussing biblical interpretation. The reason is not that Jack is hell-bent on twisting Scripture but, rather, that they are heaven-bent on understanding God's Word and applying it to their life. In fact, Jack now identifies their *former* life as being characterized by twisting Scripture. It was letting go of pleasing others that freed Jack to finally make choices based on what Jack believes God says. I wonder how many cisgender and heterosexual Christians have taken the time to study God's Word to the extent that Jack has in order to ensure that their beliefs are scriptural and not merely a product of their cisgender, heterosexual desires.

Who is the "real" Christian? Meredith or Jack? Such questions assume that we can determine a person's saving faith based purely on theological beliefs about same-sex marriage and gender identity. And yet we know that salvation is through Christ alone by faith alone through grace alone according to

Scripture alone to the glory of God alone. There is no *sola* stating "by heterosexual marriage alone" or "through celibacy alone" or "through a non-homosexual self-conception alone."[2]

Of course, people might rephrase the question to ask, "Who is the 'better' Christian?" But again, people too often assume that we can measure a person's walk with the Lord by how they define marriage and gender. What's interesting about this metric is that it ignores the fruit of the Spirit: "love, joy, peace, patience, kindness, goodness, faithfulness, gentleness, [and] self-control" (Gal. 5:22–23). Most LGBTQ people I know describe *lacking* the fruit of the Spirit prior to searching God's Word for answers. It's only when they set aside their fears and anxieties and embrace discerning their walk with the Lord that they begin to bear good fruit.

Indeed, the expectations of many churches leave LGBTQ people lonely, battling depression and anxiety, and struggling with doubts, confusion, and shame. As long as LGBTQ people remain in this place, many Christians see nothing to worry about. It's only *after* LGBTQ people start tasting a bit of happiness that many erupt in protest. Some even point to examples of good fruit and say, "See. They're happy. They clearly had ulterior motives in their choice-making." As a result, romanticized notions of "Christian suffering" attach themselves to the way LGBTQ people are expected to live.

Certainly suffering is part of the Christian life. Every Christian must take up their cross and follow Jesus (Matt. 16:24–26). However, when it comes to LGBTQ people, many Christians assume that suffering itself is the point. Living in obedience to God comes to mean nothing but hardship and struggle for LGBTQ people, and somehow this signifies their right standing in the family of God. Of course, there's nothing wrong with battling depression, anxiety, and suicidal thoughts, but few people consider that mental anguish should never be the *consequence* of a Spirit-filled theology. Any theological system that produces such fruit as a consequence of its teaching is a theological system that lacks the gospel.

When LGBTQ believers begin following their Savior according to what they believe Scripture teaches, many arrive at conclusions that produce loving relationships, joy-filled days, and internal peace. This should come as no surprise! According to Scripture, the Christian life is characterized by relational intimacy (John 13:35), joy unspeakable (1 Pet. 1:8), and peace that surpasses knowledge (Phil. 4:7). Such things don't mean that LGBTQ people aren't taking up their crosses to follow Jesus. In fact, it often means they are. "Take my yoke upon you, and learn from me," Jesus said, "and you will find *rest* for your souls" (Matt. 11:29). The cross of Jesus Christ is a burden, yes, but it is a burden that feels *light*. We exchange the oppressions of this world that weigh us *down* for a burden that lifts us *up*, foreshadowing the "eternal weight of glory beyond all comparison" (2 Cor. 4:17). "For my yoke is easy, and my burden is light" (Matt. 11:30).

Every Christian bears the weight of the yoke of Christ. But to feel the weight of that burden is to feel the weight of God's mercy and love and grace. It is to know that we belong in the family of God. That whatever wrath we might fear and whatever death we might dread is no more. That God sees us in our entirety and loves us, sends the Holy Spirit to walk beside us, takes joy in our existence the way a mother delights in her child, holds onto pictures of our littlest moments to treasure for the rest of forever.

One of my favorite C. S. Lewis quotes captures it better than I ever could: "To please God, to be a real ingredient in the divine happiness . . . to be loved by God, not merely pitied, but delighted in as an artist delights in his work or a father in a son—it seems impossible, a weight or burden of glory which our thoughts can hardly sustain. But so it is."[3]

God delights in LGBTQ people. This is our burden to bear. The weight of knowing that we are loved and accepted and affirmed as children of God that are queer and that are holy. The world has told us it's impossible. A weight or burden of glory that we've been made to believe we could never have. But so it is. And so we are.

Acknowledgments

This book wouldn't exist apart from the instrumental support I received from dear friends and family. Lauren Melissa Ellzey talked through every chapter, read my half-finished drafts, gave me feedback, and was there for me whenever I needed support. Wesley Hill gave me the push I needed to even consider a book like this in the first place, hashed out early concepts, and believed in me enough to get me started. Thomas Herrera read drafts of every chapter and gave me monthly doses of encouragement along the way. Nathan Ellzey and Kutter Callaway graciously agreed to look at different sections of the book and offer their expertise. I also owe a deep measure of gratitude to the entire team at Brazos Press for working with me and making this book a reality. Katelyn Beaty's superior editing and insightful feedback, in particular, kept me grounded throughout this entire process. Finally, every single person that I interviewed played a crucial role in shaping what I've written. I've only shared a few of their stories here. I wish I could share them all. They are some of the most amazing people I know, and I am a better person for having them in my life.

Notes

Introduction

1. "Facts about Suicide," The Trevor Project, accessed August 19, 2020, https://www.thetrevorproject.org/resources/preventing-suicide/facts-about -suicide.

2. "Facts about Suicide."

3. "LGBT Suicide Statistics in Teens," Newport Academy, May 6, 2019, https://www.newportacademy.com/resources/mental-health/lgbt-suicide -statistics.

4. "LGBT Suicide Statistics in Teens."

5. "National Estimate of LGBTQ Youth Seriously Considering Suicide" The Trevor Project, June 2019, https://www.thetrevorproject.org/wp-con tent/uploads/2019/06/Estimating-Number-of-LGBTQ-Youth-Who-Consider -Suicide-In-the-Past-Year-Final.pdf.

6. Haeyoun Park and Iaryna Mykhyalyshyn, "L.G.B.T. People Are More Likely to Be Targets of Hate Crimes Than Any Other Minority Group," *New York Times*, June 16, 2016, https://www.nytimes.com/interactive/2016/06/16 /us/hate-crimes-against-lgbt.html.

7. Harding, "Religious Faith Linked to Suicidal Behavior in LGBQ Adults," Reuters, April 13, 2018, https://tinyurl.com/5y27muec.

8. Harding, "Religious Faith Linked to Suicidal Behavior in LGBQ Adults."

9. David Kinnaman and Gabe Lyons, *unChristian: What a New Genera- tion Really Thinks about Christianity . . . and Why It Matters* (Grand Rapids: Baker Books, 2007), 92.

10. Kinnaman and Lyons, *unChristian*, 92.

Chapter 1 The Protestant Sexual Revolution

1. For a more in depth treatment of this history, see Kristin Kobes Du Mez, *Jesus and John Wayne: How White Evangelicals Corrupted a Faith*

215

and Fractured a Nation (New York: Liveright, 2020), and Ben Howe, *The Immoral Majority: Why Evangelicals Chose Political Power over Christian Values* (New York: Broadside, 2019).

2. Carl F. H. Henry, *Twilight of a Great Civilization: The Drift toward Neo-Paganism* (Westchester, IL: Crossway, 1988), 40.

3. Henry, *Twilight of a Great Civilization,* 163.

4. Henry, *Twilight of a Great Civilization,* 27.

5. Henry, *Twilight of a Great Civilization,* 41.

6. John MacArthur, "Homosexuality and the Campaign for Immorality," Grace to You, accessed February 1, 2021, https://www.gty.org/library/sermons-library/90-449.

7. Susan C. Karant-Nunn and Merry E. Wiesner, eds., *Luther on Women: A Sourcebook* (New York: Cambridge University Press, 2003), 100.

8. James A. Brundage, *Law, Sex, and Christian Society in Medieval Europe* (Chicago: University of Chicago Press, 1990), 154.

9. Brundage, *Law, Sex, and Christian Society in Medieval Europe,* 161.

10. Karant-Nunn and Wiesner, *Luther on Women,* 99.

11. Karant-Nunn and Wiesner, *Luther on Women,* 99.

12. James M. Estes, "To the Christian Nobility of the German Nation concerning the Improvement of the Christian Estate, 1520," in *The Roots of Reform,* The Annotated Luther, vol. 1, ed. Timothy J. Wengert et al. (Minneapolis: Fortress, 2015), 464.

13. Estes, "To the Christian Nobility," 426.

14. Karant-Nunn and Wiesner, *Luther on Women,* 101.

15. Estes, "To the Christian Nobility," 427.

16. William Gouge, "The First Treatise: The Scriptural Basis for Domestical Duties," in *Of Domestical Duties* (London: n.p., 1622), sec. II.II.9.

17. Richard Sibbes, *Bovvels Opened; or, A Discovery of the Neere and Deere Love, Union and Communion betwixt Christ and the Church,* 1639, http://name.umdl.umich.edu/A12167.0001.001.

18. William Whately, *A Bride-Bush; or, a Direction for Married Persons* (London: Felix Kyngston, 1619), 20.

19. Sibbes, *Bovvels Opened.*

20. Desiderius Erasmus, *In Laude and Prayse of Matrymony,* trans. Rychard Tauernour, 1536, http://name.umdl.umich.edu/A00377.0001.001.

21. Brundage, *Law, Sex, and Christian Society in Medieval Europe,* 551.

22. John Calvin, *Institutes of the Christian Religion,* trans. John Allen, 7th ed. (Philadelphia: Presbyterian Board of Christian Education, 1936), sec. 4.19.37.

23. Erik H. Herrmann, "The Babylonian Captivity of the Church," in *Church and Sacraments,* The Annotated Luther, vol. 3, ed. Paul W. Robinson et al. (Minneapolis: Fortress, 2016), 96.

24. Karant-Nunn and Wiesner, *Luther on Women,* 115.

25. Karant-Nunn and Wiesner, *Luther on Women,* 115.

26. Karant-Nunn and Wiesner, *Luther on Women,* 115.

27. Calvin, *Institutes of the Christian Religion*, sec. 4.19.37.

28. Calvin, *Institutes of the Christian Religion*, sec. 4.19.37.

29. Calvin, *Institutes of the Christian Religion*, sec. 4.19.37.

30. Karant-Nunn and Wiesner, *Luther on Women*, 147–48.

31. Karant-Nunn and Wiesner, *Luther on Women*, 105.

Chapter 2 The New Sexual Order

1. James M. Estes, "To the Christian Nobility of the German Nation Concerning the Improvement of the Christian Estate, 1520," in *The Roots of Reform*, The Annotated Luther, vol. 1, ed. Timothy J. Wengert et al. (Minneapolis: Fortress, 2015), 425.

2. Erik H. Herrmann, "The Babylonian Captivity of the Church," in *Church and Sacraments*, The Annotated Luther, vol. 3, ed. Paul W. Robinson et al. (Minneapolis: Fortress, 2016), 101.

3. Susan C. Karant-Nunn and Merry E. Wiesner, eds., *Luther on Women: A Sourcebook* (New York: Cambridge University Press, 2003), 145.

4. Karant-Nunn and Wiesner, *Luther on Women*, 101.

5. Herrmann, "Babylonian Captivity of the Church," 108.

6. Martin Luther, "Martin Luther: The Estate of Marriage," 1522, https://pages.uoregon.edu/dluebke/Reformations441/LutherMarriage.htm.

7. Steven Ozment, "Luther and the Family," *Harvard Library Bulletin* 32, no. 1 (1984): 46.

8. For "fellowship" and "companionship," see Desiderius Erasmus, *In Laude and Prayse of Matrymony*, trans. Rychard Tauernour, 1536, http://name.umdl.umich.edu/A00377.0001.001; for "love," see Leon Howard, James Barbour, and Tom Quirk, *Essays on Puritans and Puritanism* (Albuquerque: University of New Mexico Press, 1986), 154; for "joy" and "copartnership," see Thomas Gataker, *Marriage Duties Briefely Couched Togither out of Colossians*, 3. 18, 19, 1620, http://name.umdl.umich.edu/A01541.0001.001; for "conjugal affection," see Jeremy Taylor, *The Rule and Exercises of Holy Living*, 1650, https://quod.lib.umich.edu/e/eebo/A64109.0001.001?view=toc, 89; for "mutual delight," see William Gouge, "The First Treatise: The Scriptural Basis for Domestical Duties," in *Domestical Duties*, 1622, sec. II.II.9, https://chapellibrary.org:8443/pdf/books/otddu1.pdf; for "heaven on earth," see Thomas Gataker, *A Mariage Praier*, Early English Books, 1475–1640 (London: Iohn Hauiland, 1624).

9. Edmund Leites, *The Puritan Conscience and Modern Sexuality* (New Haven: Yale University Press, 1986), 95.

10. Daniel C. Maguire, *Sacred Rights: The Case for Contraception and Abortion in World Religions* (New York: Oxford University Press, 2003), 93.

11. "Very Few Americans See Contraception as Morally Wrong," Pew Research Center, September 28, 2016, https://www.pewforum.org/2016/09/28/4-very-few-americans-see-contraception-as-morally-wrong.

12. R. Albert Mohler Jr., "The Case for (Early) Marriage," Albert Mohler, August 3, 2009, https://albertmohler.com/2009/08/03/the-case-for-early-marriage.

13. R. Albert Mohler Jr., "Looking Back at 'The Mystery of Marriage'—Part Two," Albert Mohler, August 20, 2004, https://albertmohler.com/2004/08/20/looking-back-at-the-mystery-of-marriage-part-two.

14. John MacArthur, "The Scandal of the Catholic Priesthood," Grace to You, May 1, 2002, https://www.gty.org/library/sermons-library/80-264.

15. Raymond C. Ortlund, *Marriage and the Mystery of the Gospel*, Short Studies in Biblical Theology (Wheaton: Crossway, 2016), 66.

16. Ortlund, *Marriage and the Mystery of the Gospel*, 66.

17. Amy DeRogatis, *Saving Sex: Sexuality and Salvation in American Evangelicalism* (New York: Oxford University Press, 2015), 68–70.

18. Christine J. Gardner, "Of Purity Rings and Pop Stars: Using Sex to Sell Abstinence," in *Making Chastity Sexy: The Rhetoric of Evangelical Abstinence Campaigns* (Oakland: University of California Press, 2011), 44.

19. Gardner, "Of Purity Rings and Pop Stars," 47.

20. Jim Burns, *The Purity Code: God's Plan for Sex and Your Body*, Pure Foundations (Minneapolis: Bethany House, 2008), 16.

21. Dannah Gresh, *And the Bride Wore White: Seven Secrets to Sexual Purity* (Chicago: Moody, 2012), 136 (emphasis original).

22. Marshall Segal, "Have Sex Like You Know God," Desiring God, March 8, 2019, https://www.desiringgod.org/articles/have-sex-like-you-know-god.

23. Tim LaHaye and Beverly LaHaye, *The Act of Marriage: The Beauty of Sexual Love*, rev. ed. (Grand Rapids: Zondervan, 1998), 49.

24. Rob Jackson, "The Sexual-Spiritual Union of a Man and Woman," Focus on the Family, January 1, 2004, https://www.focusonthefamily.com/marriage/the-sexual-spiritual-union-of-a-man-and-woman.

25. Karant-Nunn and Wiesner, *Luther on Women*, 100.

26. Erasmus, *In Laude and Prayse of Matrymony*.

27. MacArthur, "Scandal of the Catholic Priesthood."

28. Mohler, "Case for (Early) Marriage."

29. Matthew Vines, *God and the Gay Christian: The Biblical Case in Support of Same-Sex Relationships* (New York: Convergent Books, 2015), 43.

30. Vines, *God and the Gay Christian*, 43.

31. Ortlund, *Marriage and the Mystery of the Gospel*, 66.

32. LaHaye and LaHaye, *Act of Marriage*, 49.

33. Segal, "Have Sex Like You Know God."

Chapter 3 Perverted Identity

1. Susan C. Karant-Nunn and Merry E. Wiesner, eds., *Luther on Women: A Sourcebook* (New York: Cambridge University Press, 2003), 100 (emphasis mine).

2. Karant-Nunn and Wiesner, *Luther on Women*, 100–101.

3. Ann Laura Stoler, *Race and the Education of Desire: Foucault's History of Sexuality and the Colonial Order of Things* (Durham, NC: Duke University Press, 1995).

4. Rudi Bleys, *The Geography of Perversion: Male-to-Male Sexual Behaviour outside the West and the Ethnographic Imagination, 1750–1918* (Washington Square, NY: New York University Press, 1995).

5. Bleys, *Geography of Perversion*, 191.

6. Richard von Krafft-Ebing, *Psychopathia Sexualis: With Especial Reference to the Antipathic Sexual Instinct, a Medico-Forensic Study* (New York: Rebman, 1900), 349–50.

7. Krafft-Ebing, *Psychopathia Sexualis*, 349.

8. Krafft-Ebing, *Psychopathia Sexualis*, 338.

9. Sigmund Freud, *The Interpretation of Dreams*, ed. James Strachey (New York: Basic Books, 2010).

10. Sigmund Freud, *Three Contributions to the Theory of Sex*, trans. A. A. Brill, 4th ed. (New York: Johnson, 1970).

11. Sigmund Freud, *An Outline of Psycho-Analysis*, ed. James Strachey (Mansfield Center, CT: Martino, 2010).

12. "1946," accessed September 27, 2020, https://www.1946themovie.com.

13. For more information, see Ed Oxford and Kathy Baldock, *Forging a Sacred Weapon: How the Bible Became Anti-Gay* (forthcoming).

14. Matthew Caruchet, "When the U.S. Used Lobotomies to Create Gay Auschwitz," Economic Opportunity Institute, June 27, 2019, https://www.opportunityinstitute.org/blog/post/when-the-u-s-used-lobotomies-to-create-gay-auschwitz; Peter Roger Breggin, "The Second Wave of Psychosurgery," *Mental Health* 57, nos. 10–13 (1973): 3; and Jamie Scot, "Shock the Gay Away: Secrets of Early Gay Aversion Therapy Revealed (PHOTOS)," *HuffPost*, updated December 6, 2017, https://www.huffpost.com/entry/shock-the-gay-away-secrets-of-early-gay-aversion-therapy-revealed_b_3497435.

15. "Persecution of Homosexuals in the Third Reich," United States Holocaust Memorial Museum, accessed October 25, 2020, https://encyclopedia.ushmm.org/content/en/article/persecution-of-homosexuals-in-the-third-reich.

16. Martha Vicinus, "'They Wonder to Which Sex I Belong': The Historical Roots of the Modern Lesbian Identity," *Feminist Studies* 18, no. 3 (1992): 467.

17. Quoted in James Lardner, "The War of Words," *Washington Post*, December 8, 1982, https://www.washingtonpost.com/archive/lifestyle/1982/12/08/the-war-of-words/b7c0910f-f994-407a-9e54-cc3b25972e24.

18. Howard Kurts and Charles Trueheart, "At Sacramento Union, a Conservative Bent," *Washington Post*, October 24, 1990, https://www.washingtonpost.com/archive/lifestyle/1990/10/24/at-sacramento-union-a-conservative-bent/536febcd-7bd4-4e59-be84-63dcab54ff4e.

19. Harold Hamilton, "Word Usage Offends," *Alberni Valley Times*, July 11, 2005.

20. Joseph Nicolosi, "What Freud Really Said about Homosexuality and Why," *Journal of Human Sexuality* 7 (2016): 24–42.

21. Sue Bohlin, "Homosexuality: Questions and Answers from a Biblical Perspective," Probe Ministries, May 27, 2003, https://probe.org/homosexuality-questions-and-answers.

22. Krafft-Ebing, *Psychopathia Sexualis*, 338.

23. Sunnivie Brydum, "John Paulk Formally Renounces, Apologizes for Harmful 'Ex-Gay' Movement," *The Advocate*, April 24, 2013, http://www.advocate.com/politics/religion/2013/04/24/john-paulk-formally-renounces-apologizes-harmful-ex-gay-movement.

24. James Michael Nichols, "A Survivor of Gay Conversion Therapy Shares His Chilling Story," *HuffPost*, updated November 17, 2016, https://www.huffpost.com/entry/realities-of-conversion-therapy_n_582b6cf2e4b01d8a014aea66; Katherine Ott, "The History of Getting the Gay Out," *National Museum of American History*, November 15, 2018, https://americanhistory.si.edu/blog/getting-gay-out; Jonathan Merritt, "How Christians Turned against Gay Conversion Therapy," *The Atlantic*, April 15, 2015, https://www.theatlantic.com/politics/archive/2015/04/how-christians-turned-against-gay-conversion-therapy/390570; and Jonathan Merritt, "How the Leader of the Largest Ex-Gay Ministry Dismantled the Movement," *The Atlantic*, October 6, 2015, https://www.theatlantic.com/politics/archive/2015/10/the-man-who-dismantled-the-ex-gay-ministry/408970.

25. Merritt, "How the Leader of the Largest Ex-Gay Ministry Dismantled the Movement."

26. Jonathan Merritt, "Exodus Co-Founder: I Never Saw One of Our Members Become Heterosexual," YouTube video, 1:23, posted by "exodusinternational," April 24, 2010, https://www.youtube.com/watch?v=E4dhlVYX26g.

27. Brydum, "John Paulk Formally Renounces."

28. Merritt, "How the Leader of the Largest Ex-Gay Ministry Dismantled the Movement"; and Ed Payne, "Group Apologizes to Gay Community, Shuts Down 'Cure' Ministry," CNN, updated July 8, 2013, https://www.cnn.com/2013/06/20/us/exodus-international-shutdown/index.html.

29. John Elflein, "U.S. LGBTQ Youth Who Experienced Conversion Therapy and Attempted Suicide 2020," Statista, July 21, 2020, https://www.statista.com/statistics/1053024/lgbtq-youth-in-us-attempted-suicide-conversion-therapy-experience.

30. Elflein, "U.S. LGBTQ Youth Who Experienced Conversion Therapy."

31. Jack Turban, "Gay Conversion Therapy Associated with Suicide Risk," *Psychology Today*, November 14, 2018, https://www.psychologytoday.com/blog/political-minds/201811/gay-conversion-therapy-associated-suicide-risk.

32. Anugrah Kumar, "US Appeals Court Rules Bans on Therapy for Unwanted Same-Sex Attraction Unconstitutional," *Christian Post*, November 21, 2020, https://www.christianpost.com/news/florida-therapy-bans-for-unwanted-same-sex-attraction-unconstitutional.html.

33. Karen J. Terry, John Jay College of Criminal Justice, and Catholic Church, eds., *The Causes and Context of Sexual Abuse of Minors by*

Catholic Priests in the United States, 1950–2010: A Report Presented to the United States Conference of Catholic Bishops by the John Jay College Research Team (Washington, DC: USCCB Communications, 2011); and Gregory Herek, "Facts about Homosexuality and Child Molestation," accessed September 28, 2020, https://psychology.ucdavis.edu/rainbow/html /facts_molestation.html.

34. "LGBTQ Youth and Sexual Abuse: Information for Mental Health Professionals," The National Child Traumatic Stress Network, Child Sexual Abuse Collaborative Group, 2014, https://www.nctsn.org/resources/lgbtq -youth-and-sexual-abuse-information-mental-health-professionals.

Chapter 4 Freud's Lasting Influence

1. Rosaria Champagne Butterfield, *Openness Unhindered: Further Thoughts of an Unlikely Convert on Sexual Identity and Union with Christ* (Pittsburgh: Crown & Covenant, 2015).

2. Butterfield, *Openness Unhindered*, 119.

3. Amin Ghaziani and Matt Brim, eds. *Imagining Queer Methods* (New York: New York University Press, 2019).

4. Denny Burk, *Transforming Homosexuality: What the Bible Says about Sexual Orientation and Change* (Phillipsburg, New Jersey: P&R Publishing, 2015), 34.

5. Burk, *Transforming Homosexuality*, 36.

6. Burk, *Transforming Homosexuality*, 37.

7. Ghaziani and Brim, *Imagining Queer Methods*, 282.

8. Butterfield, *Openness Unhindered*, 119.

9. Larry Kramer, *The Normal Heart* (New York: Samuel French, 2011), sec. 2.13.

10. David M. Halperin, *How to Be Gay* (Cambridge, MA: Belknap, 2012), 69.

11. Christopher Yuan, *Holy Sexuality and the Gospel: Sex, Desire, and Relationships Shaped by God's Grand Story* (Colorado Springs: Multnomah, 2018), 52.

Chapter 5 Political Christianity

1. Joshua Pease, "The Epidemic of Denial about Sexual Abuse in the Evangelical Church," *Washington Post*, May 31, 2018, https://www.washing tonpost.com/news/posteverything/wp/2018/05/31/feature/the-epidemic-of -denial-about-sexual-abuse-in-the-evangelical-church; Morgan Lee, "My Larry Nassar Testimony Went Viral. But There's More to the Gospel Than Forgiveness," *Christianity Today*, January 31, 2018, https://www.christianity today.com/ct/2018/january-web-only/rachael-denhollander-larry-nassar-for giveness-gospel.html.

2. Robert Downen, Lise Olsen, and John Tedesco, "20 Years, 700 Victims: Southern Baptist Sexual Abuse Spreads as Leaders Resist Reforms," *Houston Chronicle*, February 10, 2019, https://www.houstonchronicle.com/news

/investigations/article/Southern-Baptist-sexual-abuse-spreads-as-leaders
-13588038.php.

3. Jon Henley, "How the Boston Globe Exposed the Abuse Scandal That Rocked the Catholic Church," *The Guardian*, April 21, 2010, https://www .theguardian.com/world/2010/apr/21/boston-globe-abuse-scandal-catholic.

4. Emily C. Short, "Torts: Praying for the Parish or Preying on the Parish? Clergy Sexual Misconduct and the Tort of Clergy Malpractice," *Oklahoma Law Review* 57 (2004): 185.

5. Short, "Torts," 184.

6. Short, "Torts," 186; Garland, "Prevalence of Clergy Sexual Misconduct with Adults"; "Abuse of Power Comes as No Surprise," Not in Our Church, http://www.notinourchurch.com/statistics.html.

7. Diana R. Garland, "Prevalence of Clergy Sexual Misconduct with Adults," Baylor Social Work, https://www.baylor.edu/clergysexualmiscon duct/index.php?id=67406; "Abuse of Power Comes as No Surprise," Not in Our Church, http://www.notinourchurch.com/statistics.html.

8. Following the *Houston Chronicle*'s investigative report in 2019, some evangelical leaders did begin paying attention to the sex abuse crisis. However, as of the writing of this book, the response from most remains muted.

9. Eliott C. McLaughlin and AnneClaire Stapleton, "Tennessee Pastor Apologizes for 'Sexual Incident' with Teen," CNN, updated January 11, 2018, https://www.cnn.com/2018/01/10/us/tennessee-pastor-sexual-incident -teen-apology-applause/index.html.

10. Emily McFarlan Miller, "Jules Woodson: Andy Savage's Reported Return to Pulpit Is 'Not OK,'" *Word&Way*, October 30, 2019, https://word andway.org/2019/10/30/jules-woodson-andy-savages-reported-return-to -pulpit-is-not-ok.

11. This was the stated mission of the Revoice conference as written in 2018. The statement has been updated since then, so this no longer matches what is on their website.

12. Robert Gagnon, "Concerns with the Upcoming Revoice Conference and 'Spiritual Friendship Folk,'" *Pulpit & Pen* (blog), July 21, 2018, https:// pulpitandpen.org/2018/07/21/robert-gagnon-concerns-with-the-upcoming -revoice-conference-and-spiritual-friendship-folk.

13. Denny Burk, "What about the Revoice Conference?," *Denny Burk* (blog), May 30, 2018, https://www.dennyburk.com/what-about-the-revoice -conference.

14. R. Albert Mohler Jr., "Torn between Two Cultures? Revoice, LGBT Identity, and Biblical Christianity," Albert Mohler, August 2, 2018, https://al bertmohler.com/2018/08/02/torn-two-cultures-revoice-lgbt-identity-biblical -christianity.

15. Stanley Cohen, *Folk Devils and Moral Panics: The Creation of the Mods and Rockers*, 3rd ed. (New York: Routledge, 2002).

16. Cohen, *Folk Devils and Moral Panics*.

17. Other factors also served to unite the religious right during this time, particularly racial tension shrouded under the rhetoric of "tough on crime," "war on poverty," and "war on drugs."

18. Hans Johnson and William Eskridge, "The Legacy of Falwell's Bully Pulpit," *Washington Post*, May 19, 2007, http://www.washingtonpost.com /wp-dyn/content/article/2007/05/18/AR2007051801392.html.

19. Louis P. Sheldon and John V. Briggs, "Letters to Californians from Senator John V. Briggs and Rev. Louis P. Sheldon Requesting Support for the California Save Our Children Campaign," in California Proposition 6 Briggs Initiative Collection, 1977–1980, of ONE National Gay and Lesbian Archives, Los Angeles, Box 1, Folder 9: Briggs, John, and the Defend Our Children publicity materials 1977–1978, https://search.alexander street.com/preview/work/bibliographic_entity%7Cbibliographic_details %7C3172370.

20. Sheldon and Briggs, "Letters to Californians."

21. Johnson and Eskridge, "Legacy of Falwell's Bully Pulpit."

22. I have retold Ruth's story from various original news reports and interviews, including *Arkansas Times*, CBS, Fox News, and Katie Couric Media (KCM). See David Koon, "Ruth Coker Burks, the Cemetery Angel," *Arkansas Times*, January 8, 2015, https://arktimes.com/news/cover-stories /2015/01/08/ruth-coker-burks-the-cemetery-angel.

23. Katie Couric, "'Cemetery Angel' Ruth Coker Burks on Three Decades of Caring for AIDS Patients," KCM, June 19, 2019, https://katiecouric.com /news/2330-2/.

24. Koon, "Ruth Coker Burks"; Dustin Stephens, "The Cemetery Angel," CBS News, December 1, 2019, https://www.cbsnews.com/news/ruth-coker -burks-the-cemetery-angel/; "I Would Bury Them in Cookie Jars," Fox 16 News, November 15, 2016, https://www.fox16.com/news/i-would-bury-them -in-cookie-jars/; Couric, "'Cemetery Angel' Ruth Coker Burks"; "Jim Harwood and Ruth Coker Burks," Story Corps, accessed March 11, 2020, https:// storycorps.org/stories/jim-harwood-and-ruth-coker-burks; and "Ruth Coker Burks and Paul Wineland," Story Corps, accessed March 11, 2020, https:// storycorps.org/stories/ruth-coker-burks-and-paul-wineland.

25. Couric, "'Cemetery Angel' Ruth Coker Burks."

26. Stephens, "Cemetery Angel."

27. Couric, "'Cemetery Angel' Ruth Coker Burks."

28. Stephens, "Cemetery Angel."

29. Koon, "Ruth Coker Burks."

30. Koon, "Ruth Coker Burks."

31. Koon, "Ruth Coker Burks."

32. Koon, "Ruth Coker Burks."

33. Koon, "Ruth Coker Burks."

34. "I Would Bury Them in Cookie Jars."

35. Koon, "Ruth Coker Burks."

36. "Jim Harwood and Ruth Coker Burks."

37. "Ruth Coker Burks and Paul Wineland."

38. Stephens, "Cemetery Angel."

39. Koon, "Ruth Coker Burks."

40. Koon, "Ruth Coker Burks."

41. Koon, "Ruth Coker Burks."

42. Perry N. Halkitis, *The AIDS Generation: Stories of Survival and Resilience* (New York: Oxford University Press, 2014), 87.

43. Halkitis, *AIDS Generation*, 76.

44. Meghan Keneally, "'Friend after Friend Was Dying': HIV Survivors Look Back at Past 30 Years of AIDS in the US," ABC News, December 1, 2018, https://abcnews.go.com/Health/friend-friend-dying-hiv-survivors-back -past-30/story?id=59468714.

45. Halkitis, *AIDS Generation*, 83.

46. Halkitis, *AIDS Generation*, 89.

47. "CDC Morbidity and Mortality Weekly Report: HIV and AIDS— United States, 1981–2000," Centers for Disease Control and Prevention, accessed March 19, 2020, https://www.cdc.gov/mmwr/preview/mmwrhtml /mm5021a2.htm; and World Health Organization, ed., *The World Health Report 1999: Making a Difference* (Geneva: WHO, 1999).

48. Lawrence K. Altman, "Rare Cancer Seen in 41 Homosexuals," *New York Times*, July 3, 1981, https://www.nytimes.com/1981/07/03/us/rare-cancer -seen-in-41-homosexuals.html.

49. Mark Schoofs, "Proof Positive," *Village Voice*, July 4, 2000, https:// www.villagevoice.com/2000/07/04/proof-positive.

50. Max Fisher, "The Story of AIDS in Africa," *The Atlantic*, December 1, 2011, https://www.theatlantic.com/international/archive/2011/12/the-story -of-aids-in-africa/249361.

51. Couric, "'Cemetery Angel' Ruth Coker Burks."

Chapter 6 Hellfire and Judgment

1. David E. Anderson, "Churches Divide on AIDS," *United Press International*, December 8, 1985, https://www.upi.com/Archives/1985/12/08 /Churches-divide-on-AIDS/1915502866000.

2. Randy Frame, "Ministry: The Church's Response to Aids," *Christianity Today*, November 22, 1985, https://www.christianitytoday.com/ct/1985 /november-22/ministry-churchs-response-to-aids.html.

3. Kathy Baldock, "How I Responded to AIDS in the 1980s," *Canyonwalker Connections—LGBTQ Advocacy* (blog), November 30, 2015, http:// canyonwalkerconnections.com/responded-aids-1980s.

4. "AIDS Blamed on Acceptance of Gay Life Style," *Los Angeles Times*, January 18, 1986, https://www.latimes.com/archives/la-xpm-1986-01-18-me -953-story.html.

5. Anthony Michael Petro, *After the Wrath of God: AIDS, Sexuality, and American Religion* (Oxford: Oxford University Press, 2015), 1.

6. James L. Fletcher, "Homosexuality: Kick and Kickback," *Southern Medical Journal* 77, no. 2 (February 1984): 150.

7. Tim Fitzsimons, "LGBTQ History Month: The Early Days of America's AIDS Crisis," NBC News, October 15, 2018, https://www.nbcnews.com /feature/nbc-out/lgbtq-history-month-early-days-america-s-aids-crisis-n91 9701; and Scott Calonico, "Reagan Administration's Chilling Response to the AIDS Crisis," YouTube video, 7:43, posted by *Vanity Fair*, December 1, 2015, https://www.youtube.com/watch?v=yAzDn7tE1lU&feature=emb_logo.

8. Fitzsimons, "LGBTQ History Month"; and Calonico, "Reagan Administration's Chilling Response."

9. Editorial Team, "The History of Aids in Africa," B:M2020, August 25, 2015, https://www.blackhistorymonth.org.uk/article/section/real-stories/the -history-of-aids-in-africa.

10. Randy Frame, "Ministry: The Church's Response to Aids," *Christianity Today*, November 22, 1985, https://www.christianitytoday.com/ct /1985/november-22/ministry-churchs-response-to-aids.html.

11. United Press International, "Falwell Ordered to Pay the $5,000 He Offered," Around the Nation, *New York Times*, September 26, 1985, https:// www.nytimes.com/1985/09/26/us/around-the-nation-falwell-ordered-to-pay -the-5000-he-offered.html.

12. Jerry Falwell, *Strength for the Journey: An Autobiography* (New York: Simon & Schuster, 1987), 92–93.

13. "Fierce Controversy over Pastor's Remarks about Orlando Attack," CBS News, June 14, 2016, https://www.cbsnews.com/news/mass-shooting -orlando-gay-club-pulse-fierce-controversy-over-pastors-remarks-about -orlando-attack.

14. Sue Bohlin, "Orlando's Bizarre Coincidence?," Probe Ministries, June 29, 2016, https://probe.org/orlandos-bizarre-coincidence/.

15. R. Albert Mohler Jr., "Torn between Two Cultures? Revoice, LGBT Identity, and Biblical Christianity," Albert Mohler, August 2, 2018, https://al bertmohler.com/2018/08/02/torn-two-cultures-revoice-lgbt-identity-biblical -christianity.

16. Denny Burk, "What about the Revoice Conference?," Denny Burk, May 30, 2018, https://www.dennyburk.com/what-about-the-revoice-confer ence.

17. Robert Gagnon, "Concerns with the Upcoming Revoice Conference and 'Spiritual Friendship Folk,'" *Pulpit & Pen* (blog), July 21, 2018, https:// pulpitandpen.org/2018/07/21/robert-gagnon-concerns-with-the-upcoming -revoice-conference-and-spiritual-friendship-folk.

18. Rosaria Butterfield, "Are We Living Out Romans 1? Blessing and Curse in a Post-Obergefell World," Desiring God, February 27, 2020, https://www .desiringgod.org/articles/are-we-living-out-romans-1.

19. Albert R. Mohler, *God and the Gay Christian? A Response to Matthew Vines* (Louisville: Southern Baptist Theological Seminary Press, 2014), 37.

Chapter 7 Culture and Context

1. The word *eisegetical* refers to reading our own worldview into the text.

2. Amanda Montell, *Wordslut: A Feminist Guide to Taking Back the English Language* (New York: Harper Wave, 2019), 21–27.

3. William Shakespeare, "Romeo and Juliet," The Folger Shakespeare, Act 3, scene 1, lines 118–20, https://shakespeare.folger.edu/shakespeares-works /romeo-and-juliet.

4. Wayne R. Dynes, Warren Johansson, William A. Percy, and Stephen Donaldson, eds., *Encyclopedia of Homosexuality*, Garland Reference Library of Social Science (New York: Garland, 1990), 348.

5. David M. Halperin, *How to Do the History of Homosexuality* (Chicago: University of Chicago Press, 2002), 111.

6. Craig A. Williams, *Roman Homosexuality: Ideologies of Masculinity in Classical Antiquity* (New York: Oxford University Press, 1999).

7. Judith P. Hallett and Marilyn B. Skinner, eds., *Roman Sexualities* (Princeton: Princeton University Press, 1997); Myles McDonnell, *Roman Manliness: Virtus and the Roman Republic* (New York: Cambridge University Press, 2006).

8. Sarah Ruden, *Paul among the People: The Apostle Reinterpreted and Reimagined in His Own Time* (New York: Image Books, 2011), 46.

9. Ruden, *Paul among the People*, 46. See also Hallett and Skinner, *Roman Sexualities*.

10. "Report of the Ad Interim Committee on Human Sexuality," General Assembly of the Presbyterian Church in America, May 2020, https://pcaga .org/aicreport; and Bridget Eileen Rivera, "A Christian Response to the PCA Report on Human Sexuality," *Meditations* (blog), June 10, 2020, https://www .meditationsofatravelingnun.com/a-christian-response-to-the-pca-report-on -human-sexuality.

Chapter 8 Double Standards

1. Daniel C. Maguire, *Sacred Rights: The Case for Contraception and Abortion in World Religions* (New York: Oxford University Press, 2003), 87.

2. Allan C. Carlson, *Godly Seed: American Evangelicals Confront Birth Control, 1873–1973* (New Brunswick: Transaction, 2012).

3. Carlson, *Godly Seed*.

4. John Calvin, *Commentaries on the First Book of Moses Called Genesis*, vol. 2, trans. Rev. John King, Christian Classics Ethereal Library, http://bts freeccm.org/pluginfile.php/22856/mod_resource/content/5/Calvin%20Com mentary%20Genesis%20vol.%202.pdf, 241.

5. John Wesley, *John Wesley's Notes on the Bible*, https://ccel.org/ccel /wesley/notes/notes.ii.ii.xxxix.ii.html.

6. Martin Luther, *Luther's Works*, vol. 7, *Lectures on Genesis: Chapters 38–44*, ed. Jaroslav Jan Pelikan, Walter A. Hansen, and Helmut T. Lehmann (St. Louis: Concordia, 1965), chap. 38.

7. Luther, *Luther's Works*, vol. 7, chap. 38.

8. Clement of Alexandria, *The Fathers of the Church*, vol. 3, *Christ the Educator*, trans. Simon P. Wood (Washington, DC: Catholic University of America Press, 2010), 167.

9. Clement of Alexandria, *Fathers of the Church*, 3:170.

10. Augustine, "On Marriage and Concupiscence (Book I)," New Advent, https://www.newadvent.org/fathers/15071.htm, chap. 17.

11. Jerome, *The Letters of St. Jerome*, trans. W. H. Fremantle, G. Lewis, and W. G. Martley (Aeterna, 2016), 43.

12. Epiphanius, *The Panarion of Epiphanius of Salamis: Book I (Sects. 1–46)*, 2nd ed., trans. Frank Williams (Boston: Brill, 2009), 26:19, 3.

13. Clement of Alexandria, *Fathers of the Church*, 3:169, 170 (emphasis mine).

14. "Contraceptive Use in the United States," Guttmacher Institute, April 2020, https://www.guttmacher.org/fact-sheet/contraceptive-use-united-states.

15. Historically, the word *celibate* simply meant *unmarried*. However, in this book, I've decided to use the word *celibate* as it is colloquially understood today, referring to anyone who chooses to abstain from sexual relations, whether married or unmarried.

16. John Piper, "Divorce & Remarriage: A Position Paper," Desiring God, July 21, 1986, https://www.desiringgod.org/articles/divorce-and-remarriage-a-position-paper.

17. Gordon J. Wenham and William E. Heth, *Jesus and Divorce* (Eugene, OR: Wipf & Stock, 2010).

18. Wenham and Heth, *Jesus and Divorce*.

19. Piper, "Divorce & Remarriage."

20. Piper, "Divorce & Remarriage" (emphasis mine).

21. Bethlehem Church, "A Statement on Divorce & Remarriage in the Life of Bethlehem Baptist Church," Desiring God, May 2, 1989, https://www.desiringgod.org/articles/a-statement-on-divorce-and-remarriage-in-the-life-of-bethlehem-baptist-church.

22. Eliana Dockterman, "5 Things Women Need to Know about the Hobby Lobby Ruling," *Time*, July 1, 2014, https://time.com/2941323/supreme-court-contraception-ruling-hobby-lobby; and Adam Liptak, "Supreme Court Uphold Trump Administration Regulation Letting Employers Opt Out of Birth Control Coverage," *New York Times*, July 8, 2020, https://www.nytimes.com/2020/07/08/us/supreme-court-birth-control-obamacare.html.

23. "Contraceptive Use in the United States."

Chapter 9 Effeminacy

1. Byrne R. S. Fone, *Homophobia: A History* (New York: Picador, 2001), 319–20.

2. Fone, *Homophobia*, 316.

3. See Fone, *Homophobia*.

4. Myles Anthony McDonnell, *Roman Manliness: Virtus and the Roman Republic* (New York: Cambridge University Press, 2006).

5. Michèle Cohen, "'Manners' Make the Man: Politeness, Chivalry, and the Construction of Masculinity, 1750–1830," *Journal of British Studies* 44, no. 2 (April 2005): 312–29.

6. John Eldredge, *Wild at Heart: Discovering the Secret of a Man's Soul* (Nashville: Nelson, 2001), 10–11.

7. Eldredge, *Wild at Heart,* 67.

8. Eldredge, *Wild at Heart,* 8.

9. Robert Lewis, *Raising a Modern-Day Knight: A Father's Role in Guiding His Son to Authentic Manhood* (Carol Stream, IL: Tyndale, 2007).

10. Stu Weber, *Tender Warrior: Every Man's Purpose, Every Woman's Dream, Every Child's Hope* (Sisters, OR: Multnomah, 2006).

11. Colin Smothers, "The Abolition of Men?," CBMW, August 12, 2019, https://cbmw.org/topics/men/the-abolition-of-men.

12. "Born to Be Brave," accessed February 3, 2020, http://borntobebrave.com.

13. Greg Morse, "Grooming the Next Generation: Did Gillette Miss a Spot?," Desiring God, January 18, 2019, https://www.desiringgod.org/articles/grooming-the-next-generation.

14. Greg Morse, "Play the Man You Are: Will Effeminacy Keep Anyone from Heaven?," Desiring God, February 5, 2019, https://www.desiringgod.org/articles/play-the-man-you-are.

15. Morse, "Play the Man You Are."

16. Morse, "Grooming the Next Generation."

17. Morse, "Play the Man You Are."

18. Kevin DeYoung, "Play the Man," *The Gospel Coalition* (blog), July 26, 2011, https://www.thegospelcoalition.org/blogs/kevin-deyoung/play-the-man.

19. John Piper and Wayne A. Grudem, eds., *Recovering Biblical Manhood and Womanhood: A Response to Evangelical Feminism* (Wheaton: Crossway, 1991), 309.

20. Piper and Grudem, *Recovering Biblical Manhood and Womanhood,* 309.

21. Piper and Grudem, *Recovering Biblical Manhood and Womanhood,* 309.

22. Piper and Grudem, *Recovering Biblical Manhood and Womanhood,* 309–10.

Chapter 10 Emasculation

1. Leslie Ludy, *Set-Apart Femininity* (Eugene, OR: Harvest House, 2008), 29.

2. Ludy, *Set-Apart Femininity,* 28.

3. Nancy Leigh DeMoss, ed., "Portrait of a True Woman," in *Becoming God's True Woman,* 2nd ed. (Wheaton: Crossway, 2008), 63–78.

4. Carolyn Mahaney, "Femininity: Developing a Biblical Perspective," in DeMoss, *Becoming God's True Woman*, 26–27.

5. John Eldredge and Stasi Eldredge, *Captivating: Unveiling the Mystery of a Woman's Soul* (Nashville: Nelson, 2005), 158.

6. Caroline Blyth, Emily Colgan, and Katie B. Edwards, eds., *Rape Culture, Gender Violence, and Religion: Christian Perspectives* (Cham, Switzerland: Palgrave Macmillan, 2018), 9.

7. John Piper and Wayne A. Grudem, eds., *Recovering Biblical Manhood and Womanhood: A Response to Evangelical Feminism* (Wheaton: Crossway, 1991), 36.

8. Piper and Grudem, *Recovering Biblical Manhood and Womanhood*, 28–29.

9. Aimee Byrd, *Recovering from Biblical Manhood and Womanhood: How the Church Needs to Rediscover Her Purpose* (Grand Rapids: Zondervan, 2020), 22; see also John Piper, "Should Women Be Police Officers?," Desiring God, August 13, 2015, https://www.desiringgod.org/interviews /should-women-be-police-officers; and Piper and Grudem, *Recovering Biblical Manhood and Womanhood*, 41–42.

10. Mahaney, "Femininity," in DeMoss, *Becoming God's True Woman*, 26–27.

11. Daniel Silliman and Kate Shellnutt, "Ravi Zacharias Hid Hundreds of Pictures of Women, Abuse during Massages, and a Rape Allegation," *Christianity Today*, February 11, 2021, https://www.christianitytoday.com/news/2021 /february/ravi-zacharias-rzim-investigation-sexual-abuse-sexting-rape.html.

12. Quoted in Byrd, *Recovering from Biblical Manhood and Womanhood*, 22.

13. Roderick A. Ferguson, *Aberrations in Black: Toward a Queer of Color Critique* (Minneapolis: University of Minnesota Press, 2004).

Chapter 11 Gender Essentialism

1. Plato, *The Republic*, trans. Benjamin Jowett (Minneapolis: First Avenue Editions, 2015).

2. Plato, *Timeaus*, trans. W. R. M. Lamb, Plato in Twelve Volumes (London: Harvard University Press, 1925), 9:42a.

3. Aristotle, *Generation of Animals*, trans. A. L. Peck (Cambridge, MA: Harvard University Press, 1942), sec. 767b.

4. Aristotle, "Generation of Animals," sec. 767b.

5. Aristotle, "Generation of Animals," sec. 768a.

6. Aristotle, "Politics," trans. H. Rackham (Cambridge, MA: Harvard University Press, 1932), sec. 1254b.

7. Rachel Green Miller, *Beyond Authority and Submission: Women and Men in Marriage, Church, and Society* (Phillipsburg, NJ: P&R, 2019), 50.

8. Judith P. Hallett and Marilyn B. Skinner, eds., *Roman Sexualities* (Princeton: Princeton University Press, 1997), 29–44.

9. Mark J. Adair, "Plato's View of the 'Wandering Uterus,'" *Classical Journal* 91, no. 2 (1995): 153–63.

10. Helene P. Foley, *Female Acts in Greek Tragedy*, Martin Classical Lectures (Princeton, NJ: Princeton University Press, 2001), 333.

11. Foley, *Female Acts in Greek Tragedy*, 333.

12. Sarah Ruden, *Paul among the People: The Apostle Reinterpreted and Reimagined in His Own Time* (New York: Image Books, 2011), 81.

13. Ruden, *Paul among the People*, 96.

Chapter 12 More Than Just Monkeys?

1. Jack has related their story in more detail on Twitter. See Jonathan "Jack" Bates (@jackmb), "So I know this happens in the ACNA," Twitter, March 4, 2021, 5:59 p.m., https://twitter.com/jackmb/status/1367610566869544960?s=21; Jonathan "Jack" Bates (@jackmb), "So I was kicked out of theology school one time," Twitter, May 19, 2020, 8:30 p.m., https://twitter.com/jackmb/status/1262903462318223362?s=21.

2. Amy Elizabeth Ansell, *Race and Ethnicity: The Key Concepts* (New York: Routledge, 2013), 21.

3. Quoted in Sandra Lipsitz Bem, *The Lenses of Gender: Transforming the Debate on Sexual Inequality* (New Haven: Yale University Press, 1993), 10.

4. Essentialist arguments were also used to rebut the successes of the Black Civil Rights, Gay Rights, and Disability Rights movements.

5. Lionel Tiger, "The Possible Biological Origins of Sexual Discrimination," *Maryland Law Forum* 1 (1970): 2; and Bem, *Lenses of Gender*, 14.

6. Edward O. Wilson, *Sociobiology: The New Synthesis* (1975; repr., Cambridge, MA: Belknap, 2000); and Edward O. Wilson, *On Human Nature* (1979; Cambridge, MA: Harvard University Press, 2004).

7. Bem, *Lenses of Gender*, 17–18.

8. I often heard this in my childhood, and the saying was based on Kevin Johnson and James R. White's *What's with the Mutant in the Microscope?* (Minneapolis: Bethany House, 1999).

9. Matt Moore, "How I Discovered True Masculinity," The Gospel Coalition, April 27, 2016, https://www.thegospelcoalition.org/article/how-i-discovered-true-masculinity.

10. As the conversation unfolded and I pressed him further, Buck eventually retreated from his original stance and instead asserted that the word *masculine* is unhelpful and that he preferred to speak only in terms of being a "man of God." After this, it became unclear what he was trying to argue.

11. John Piper and Wayne A. Grudem, eds., *Recovering Biblical Manhood and Womanhood: A Response to Evangelical Feminism* (Wheaton: Crossway, 1991), 21–22.

12. Heath Lambert, "Talking to Your Children about Transgenderism," The Council on Biblical Manhood and Womanhood, June 1, 2017, https://cbmw.org/2017/06/01/talking-to-your-children-about-transgenderism.

13. Robert A. J. Gagnon, "Transsexuality and Ordination," August 2007, https://strateias.org/transsexuality.pdf, 13.

14. Piper and Grudem, *Recovering Biblical Manhood and Womanhood*, 287.

15. Piper and Grudem, *Recovering Biblical Manhood and Womanhood*, 286.

16. John Piper, "Is Modesty an Issue in the Church Today?," Desiring God, November 19, 2007, https://www.desiringgod.org/interviews/is-modesty-an-issue-in-the-church-today.

17. Kevin DeYoung, "The Lost Virtue of Modesty," *The Gospel Coalition* (blog), October 2, 2014, https://www.thegospelcoalition.org/blogs/kevin-deyoung/the-biblical-virtue-of-modesty.

18. Austen Hartke, *Transforming: The Bible and the Lives of Transgender Christians* (Louisville: Westminster John Knox, 2018), 33.

Chapter 13 Vessels of Wrath

1. In this context, "gender conformity" is when a person fits or "conforms" to status-quo expectations related to gender.

2. Matthias Roberts, *Beyond Shame: Creating a Healthy Sex Life on Your Own Terms* (Minneapolis: Fortress, 2020), 19.

3. Rebecca Randall, "Wayne Grudem Changes Mind about Divorce in Cases of Abuse," *Christianity Today*, November 26, 2019, https://www.christianitytoday.com/news/2019/november/complementarian-wayne-grudem-ets-divorce-after-abuse.html.

Chapter 14 Grace for Me but Not for Thee

1. While it's true that LGBTQ issues are not remotely comparable to issues like rape, murder, and molestation, it's worth noting that Christians do indeed have a history of defending the salvation of people who engaged in and defended such practices. The most salient examples are Christian slave masters from the sixteenth to nineteenth centuries. These men either personally engaged in slave-holding—a practice that included institutionalized rape, molestation, and horrendous examples of physical violence and murder—or defended the institutions that upheld it. Most never repented in the span of their lifetimes. Many Christians nevertheless defend their salvation and uphold them as models of spiritual maturity. Jonathan Edwards and George Whitefield are notable examples.

Chapter 15 Recentering the Gospel

1. Mark Woods, "Burned at the Stake, Racked and Drowned: Why Did Everyone Hate the Anabaptists?," *Christianity Today*, March 10, 2016, https://www.christiantoday.com/article/burned-at-the-stake-racked-and-drowned-why-did-everyone-hate-the-anabaptists/81608.htm.

2. Tal Howard, "Charisma and History: The Case of Münster, Westphalia, 1534–1535," *Essays in History* 35 (1993): 48–64.

3. "The Historic Baptist Church at Monksthorpe 1701," accessed August 25, 2020, https://www.monksthorpe.com.

4. "Posture Shift—Bill Henson," YouTube video, 1:41:13, posted by Valley Christian Center, June 6, 2018, https://www.youtube.com/watch?v=ErFz_rzAmWw.

Chapter 16 Setting Down the Burdens

1. Erik H. Herrmann, "The Babylonian Captivity of the Church," in *Church and Sacraments*, The Annotated Luther, vol. 3, ed. Paul W. Robinson et al. (Minneapolis: Fortress, 2016), 101.

Chapter 17 Weights of Glory

1. Visit the website for the It Gets Better Project here: https://itgetsbetter.org.

2. The five *solas* of the Reformation are a set of foundational principles developed by reformers to correct theological error in the Catholic Church.

3. C. S. Lewis, *Weight of Glory* (New York: HarperOne, 2009), 22.

Author Bio

Bridget Eileen Rivera writes and speaks on faith, sexuality, and justice. Her website, Meditations of a Traveling Nun, is a leading resource on gay celibacy, attracting thousands of visitors every month. She has worked with a number of faith-based organizations, including Revoice, Christians for Social Action, and Preston Sprinkle's Center for Faith, Sexuality & Gender, where she contributed to the Digital Leaders Forum. Rivera is currently pursuing her PhD in sociology from the City University of New York Graduate Center. You can follow her on social media at @travelingnun.